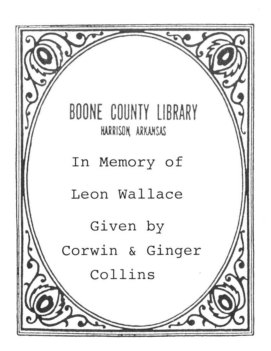

STOREY'S GUIDE TO

Feeding
Horses

STOREY'S GUIDE TO

Feeding Horses

LIFELONG NUTRITION ◆ FEED STORAGE
FEEDING TIPS ◆ PASTURE MANAGEMENT

MELYNI WORTH

Storey Publishing

The mission of Storey Publishing is to serve our customers by publishing practical information that encourages personal independence in harmony with the environment.

Edited by Deborah Burns and Sue Ducharme
Art direction by Meredith Maker
Cover design by Meredith Maker
Cover photograph © Gemma Giannini from Grant Heilman
    Photography, Inc.
Illustrations by JoAnna Rissanen
Text production by Jennifer Jepson Smith
Indexed by Jan Williams

Printed in the United States by Malloy
10 9 8 7 6 5 4 3 2 1

Library of Congress Cataloging-in-Publication Data
Worth, Melyni.
    Storey's guide to feeding horses / Melyni Worth.
        p. cm.
    ISBN 1-58017-496-5 (alk. paper) — ISBN 1-58017-492-2 (pbk. : alk.
paper)
    1. Horses—Feeding and feeds. 2. Horses—Nutrition. I. Title: Guide
to feeding horses. II. Title: Feeding horses. III. Title.
SF285.5 .W67 2004
636.1'085—dc22
                            2003014940

Contents

ABBREVIATIONS USED IN THIS BOOK

AA	Amino acid
ACTH	Adreno Cortico-Stimulating Hormone
ADF	Acid detergent fiber (Van Soest measure of indigestible fiber)
ATP	Adenosine triphosphate, energy carrier within the cell
BW	Body weight (of the horse)
CHO	Carbohydrates, usually means simple carbs like starch and sugar
CP	Crude Protein (measure of protein supplied based on nitrogen content)
DOD	Degenerative Joint Disease (erosion of cartilage in joints due to OCD)
DM	Dry Matter (weight after all water has been removed)
EE	Ether extract (measure of fat content)
EFAs	Essential Fatty Acids, special polyunsaturated fats that are needed in the diet
EPSM	Equine Polysaccharide Storage Myopathy (disease of muscle)
GE	Gross energy (of feed)
GI	Gastrointestinal tract
HYPP	HyperKalemic Periodic Paralysis
Mcal	Megacalories =1,000 Kcal
Mg/kg	Milligrams per kilogram, same as ppm
NDF	Neutral detergent fiber (Van Soest measure of digestible fiber)
NRC	National Research Council
NSC	Non-Structural Carbohydrates (starch and sugar content of the plant)
OCD	Osteochondrosis dissecans (Malformation of bone underlying joint surface)
Ppm	Parts per million, same as mg/kg
RER	Recurrent Exerional Rhabdomyolysis (a form of tying up)
SI	Small intestine, where enzymic digestion takes place
TDN	Total Digestible Nutrients
TDS	Total Dissolved Salts, a measure of water quality
VFAs	Volatile Fatty Acids, the fats the bacteria in the hind gut produce as a waste product utilized by the horse

-1-

Basics of
Equine Digestion

THE EARLIEST ANCESTOR OF THE HORSE was a forest-dwelling, dog-sized, browsing mammal known as *Eohippus*. Over millions of years, on the open plains of North America, the modern equine we call *Equus caballus* evolved as a roaming, grazing animal. Herds of horses traveled from water hole to water hole, grazing on the tough native grasses as they walked. They covered long distances, 25 or more miles per day, and ultimately they wandered right off the continent.

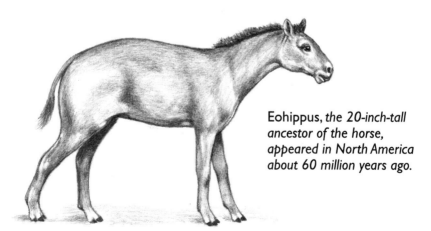

Eohippus, the 20-inch-tall ancestor of the horse, appeared in North America about 60 million years ago.

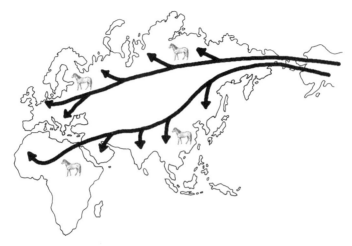

Wandering westward across the Bering Land Bridge during the ice ages, horses left North America and populated Asia, Europe, and Africa.

During the various ice ages, at least four separate migrations of horses passed over the Bering Land Bridge from North America into Asia. Once there, the horses kept moving west and south, until the various sub-species of *Equus* had established themselves in Asia, Europe, and Africa. The last migrations occurred roughly 9,000 years ago. After the Bering Land Bridge disappeared about 1,000 years later, the horse, along with the sloth and the mastodon, became totally extinct in North America. No one knows exactly why.

Herds of horses grazed and wandered the plains, covering long distances between watering holes and eating the tough, stemmy grasses.

Nature's Plan for Feeding Horses

When European explorers eventually reintroduced horses to North America, the animals adapted well to the environment that had originally shaped them. Horses are herbivores: that is, they eat only plants. They never hunt or eat prey and in fact were themselves prey animals for the large carnivores.

The range plants that they ate were sparse and often very fibrous, containing in their cell walls large amounts of hard-to-digest cellulose. The only time of the year that grasses were high in sugar was the early spring, and then only for a few weeks. After grasses flower and go to seed in the summer, the stalks and stems remain, containing very little, if any, sugar.

The sugar solution contained within the plant cells is easily digested in the equine stomach and small intestine, but, like all mammals, the horse does not have the digestive enzymes required to breakdown cellulose, the material that makes up cell walls. The bonds that form the cellulose branches, called beta-glycan or beta-glucan links, can be broken only by bacteria.

To process the large amounts of cellulose, the equine digestive system evolved to include three large fermentation sacs: the cecum and the ventral and dorsal colons. In these sacs, the fibrous remains of the grasses mix with a population of digestive bacteria that are able to break down the cell walls and convert them to energy. The bacteria give off fatty acids as a waste product of this degradation of cellulose. The walls of the colons are able to absorb the fatty acids, which the horse can then utilize for energy metabolism via the liver. (See pages 7–14 for more on the digestive process.)

Thus horses evolved to live on a low-energy diet, grazing all day long, moving gently all the time. Speed was reserved for emergencies such as running away from a predator. They took in food continuously; it required much chewing and was low in sugar and high in fibrous, hard-to-digest nutrients.

Carbohydrate ABCs

Although all sugars are carbohydrates, not all carbohydrates are sugars. Carbohydrates are a complex family of molecules that are produced by plants from the base molecule glucose and other simple sugars. How they are digested by the horse depends on how complex the molecule is, which in turn depends on where the plant is in its life cycle when eaten by the horse.

From Sunlight to Sugar

As grasses (and other plants) grow, they use energy from sunlight to produce simple sugars from water and the carbon dioxide (CO_2) in the air. The sugars are then bound together into chains called starches. As the starches accumulate, the plant binds them into longer chains called hemi-celluloses.

As the plant grows, it joins the hemi-cellulose molecules together, binding them with beta-glycan linkage into branching chains known as cellulose. Cellulose becomes the building material for cell walls. (See diagram on page 25.)

As the plant matures, cellular walls must become stronger and firmer. To accomplish this, the plant starts to bind nitrogen into the cellulose. Nitrogen (which comes from the air or the roots) is bound irreversibly to the cellulose to form the component lignin. Lignin provides the cell walls with rigidity and supportive strength.

The order of digestibility of the various stages of plant material is: sugar, starch, hemi-cellulose, cellulose, and lignin. Thus as the plant ages, progressively less digestible material is produced.

Humans do not possess a sufficiently large fermentation organ to extract more than a minimal supply of energy from botanical cell walls. To us, cellulose is non-digestible fiber and passes through. The ability — or otherwise — to access energy from cellulose is a central difference between omnivores, like humans, and herbivores. To the horse and other herbivores, cellulose is a valuable source of energy, because their gastrointestinal (GI) bacteria are able to break it down into glucose.

An interesting fact for your trivia collection: The only animals that can break down the nitrogen-carbon bonds of lignin are termites. So even to herbivores, including the horse, lignin is a non-digestible fiber.

How digestible any given plant material is depends on the percentage of lignin it contains. Because lignin is produced as the plant progresses through its growth cycle, the amount present depends on the age or stage of development of the plant at the time it is either eaten or harvested. The more mature the plant, the higher the percentages of cellulose and lignin.

Thus spring grasses at an early stage of growth are high in sugars — and dangerous to insulin-resistant horses and other horses with a tendency to founder. Grasses produce increasing amounts of cellulose and subsequently lignin, so as they mature, this danger diminishes. After they have bloomed and seeded, grasses die back, leaving only the lignified skeleton, which is almost totally indigestible.

Cereal plants (wheat, barley, and rye) are varieties of grasses and follow the same pattern. By the time they are harvested for the seeds (grains), their stalks are almost entirely lignin. Even though they are cut much earlier in their growth cycle when they are cut for hay, they still tend to have a lot of lignin in their strong stalks. Hence the tendency for the cereal hays (oat hay, barley hay) to be indigestible to a horse younger than one year old. An adult, with its much bigger GI tract, can handle such hays, but most babies can't.

Domestication Brought Drastic Changes

When humans domesticated the horse for the purposes of agriculture, transportation, sport, and war, the horse's natural lifestyle was considerably altered. Horses no longer had time to wander and graze. For human convenience and to accommodate equine work schedules, feed was provided in a few separate meals before and after work. Horses had to work hard and often move fast, expending increased energy. In order to supply these higher energy demands, humans fed horses starch-rich cereal grains.

It has been suggested that the practice of feeding grain to warhorses started around 859 B.C. with the Assyrians, who fed barley to give their chariot ponies more energy and enable them to gallop faster and longer. Grain feeding most probably started with horses used by the military and was slower to be introduced to horses used for agriculture or transportation. We do know that Xenophon was well acquainted with feeding grain to warhorses in the fourth century A.D., as were the Romans. But the practice of feeding grain certainly developed after humans left behind a nomadic lifestyle and an agriculture base was established.

Barley was the first domesticated cereal grain. Warhorses were reputedly fed a mash of ground barley the night before battle to supply extra energy. Over time, oats and corn were added to the menu. Wheat and rice were too valuable as human food to use for horses, although bran, a by-product of wheat milling, was used for many centuries to feed horses.

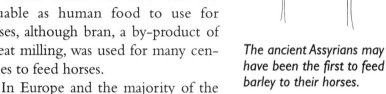

The ancient Assyrians may have been the first to feed barley to their horses.

In Europe and the majority of the western world, the horses used for transportation and agriculture were housed in limited space. This represented another considerable lifestyle change for the horse. Before the invention of the internal combustion engine, horses supplied the main power for transportation; many thousands of them were kept in stables in cities and towns. During this period, most horses lost all access to natural grazing.

Many of our traditional horse-keeping methods derive from these times. Indeed, many horse-keeping practices in North America came over with the colonists. Today, in Europe and in urban areas of the United States, where land — especially pasture land — is less available, horses are often housed in limited areas and in stables.

A large number of our modern equine management problems (such as colic, cribbing, founder, tying-up, and bad behavior) are a direct result of both the removal of the horse from its original environment and the lifestyle changes that have made most horses dependent on humans for their care and feeding. We could prevent a majority of these common problems if we allowed horses to live more naturally; that is, out in a pasture in groups, walking around eating grasses.

Horses would also be much better off if we didn't feed them so much cereal grain. While the feeding of grain to horses has historical precedent and came about for practical reasons at the time when horses were the main means of transportation and motive power, benefits have not come without a price. Certainly we don't see the problems of cribbing, founder, and tying-up in feral horses. (See Chapter 8 for information on feeding-related problems.)

How The Horse Digests Its Food

The horse is blessed with an unusual digestive tract. With ruminant herbivores such as cattle and sheep, digestion begins in the large double sac called the reticulo-rumen. In contrast, the horse's gastrointestinal (GI) tract resembles a pig's. Its small simple stomach and small intestine lead to giant sacs where bacterial fermentation takes place. Many of the horse's special requirements are because of this unusual digestive arrangement.

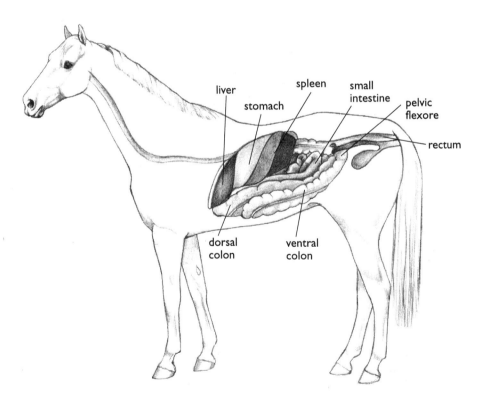

The equine gastrointestinal tract fills most of the peritoneal cavity. This shows the left side.

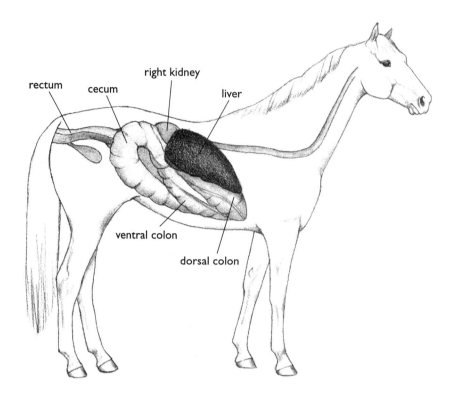

The equine gastrointestinal tract: right side.

Mouth

The mouth is used to gather food and chew it to break down cell walls, then to mix the food with saliva, which contains the enzyme amylase. The amylase begins the process of breaking down starches. Saliva also contains mucin, a slippery protein that acts as a lubricant to aid passage of food down the esophagus, to the stomach.

Equine teeth are brachydonty, a term which means that they are very long and deeply rooted in the jaws. They grow out steadily over the horse's adult lifespan and are worn down at the grinding surface as the horse chews. The upper jaw is wider than the lower jaw, and because the horse chews with a side-to-side motion, each tooth is ground down by the opposing tooth. If a tooth is lost, however, the opposing one will not be ground down and will continue to grow. Such a tooth can become so long that it prevents the sideways movement of the jaw or can even prevent the jaw from closing. This can mean that the horse cannot chew its food properly or drops food because of the discomfort of trying to chew. This loss of ability to chew food properly can cause a host of health and behavior problems, ranging from weight loss, colic, and foul breath to bitting and training issues.

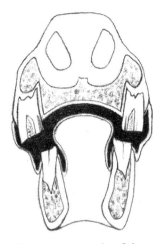

The upper arcade of the teeth is wider than the lower.

The outside edge of the upper teeth and the inside edge of the lower teeth are not adequately ground down in the chewing process. These tend to develop long "hooks" or sharp edges, which can cut the inside of the cheeks or the tongue. It is important for the health and comfort of the mouth and efficient chewing and digestion that the sharp hooks or edges are removed, which is best accomplished by a suitably qualified professional, usually a veterinarian with dental training and power tools, in a procedure called floating. A hand-powered rasp is not sufficient to level teeth properly.

Stomach

Unlike most other herbivorous livestock, the horse's stomach is very small relative to its size — only about twice the size of the human stomach, which is small for an animal that is generally ten times the body weight of a human. Cattle and sheep, for example, have huge, multi-chambered stomachs (reticulo-rumen), but the horse has a simple stomach.

The stomach walls excrete hydrochloric acid and the enzyme trypsin. This combination of acid and enzyme initiates the process of breaking down proteins. The walls of the stomach are covered with thick mucus to prevent the acid and enzyme mixture from eating away at the stomach lining.

In essence, the stomach is a holding and mixing chamber. Except for glucose, the mucus-lined walls are not suitable for absorption. The rest of the nutrients are slowly digested as the food sits in the stomach and begins to move down the small intestine. It is the small intestine where most of the absorption of the digested food occurs.

In some areas, the protective mucus layer is normally thinner, and in these places excess acid can damage the stomach walls, contributing to ulcers. Large meals that overfill the stomach will also tend to lead to the development of ulcers, especially if the food is high in sugar and starch.

Small Intestine

As food exits the stomach and enters the small intestine, it is mixed with various enzymes, and gradually the mixture becomes more alkaline, or less acidic.

Carbohydrate Digestion

It is here that the bulk of the readily soluble carbohydrates (starch and sugars) are broken down to simple sugars. The sugars cross the small intestine wall and are absorbed into the bloodstream. All the blood cells carrying sugar from the small intestine are collected in a

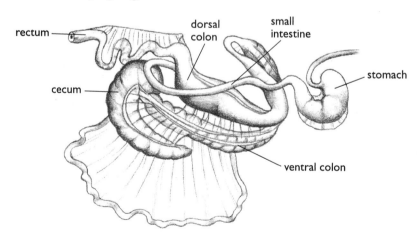

The equine intestines in a simplified view. Note the three large fermentation sacs (the cecum and the two colons).

GLYCEMIC RESPONSE

When the horse digests simple carbohydrates like starch and sugar, they are broken down to glucose and other simple sugars. These are absorbed into the bloodstream, causing an elevation in blood sugar, which triggers release of the hormone insulin in direct response to the amount and presence of sugar in the bloodstream. This is called the glycemic response. The degree to which the insulin level rises depends on the amount of glucose that the meal produces. The insulin causes the muscle and other cells to absorb the sugar from the bloodstream and hence lowers the blood sugar.

blood vessel called the hepatic portal vein, which transports it to the liver.

The pancreas releases the hormone insulin in direct response to the amount and presence of sugar in the bloodstream. This is called the glycemic response. Insulin causes the muscles and other cells to absorb the sugar from the bloodstream and hence lowers the blood sugar. The degree to which the insulin level rises depends on the amount of glucose that the meal produces.

When the horse digests simple carbohydrates like starch and sugar, they are broken down to glucose and other simple sugars. These are absorbed into the bloodstream.

Fat Digestion

The digesta (food being digested) is combined in the small intestine with both bile salts that flow almost continuously from the liver and with an enzyme called lipase. The bile salts and lipase emulsify the fats (allow them to be mixable with water), which then form little balls called chylomicra. These chylomicra cross the walls of the small intestine and are collected into the lymph system. The lymph carrying the chylomicra flows to the big lymph glands in the neck, where they enter the bloodstream.

Protein Digestion

Pancreatic enzymes are secreted into the GI tract and continue the process of breaking down the protein. The big protein molecules are broken into individual amino acids and short chains of simple amino acids called polypeptides, and then they are absorbed across the cell walls into the bloodstream. The polypeptides and amino acids pass to the liver, where they are sorted and used for the generation of important proteins or are bound and sent via the bloodstream to the tissues where they are needed.

Hind-Gut: Digestion By Bacterial Fermentation

Once the digesta has moved through the small intestine, most of the soluble portions have been removed. The remains, which are

A DELICATE BALANCE: HORSE AND GUT BACTERIA

The horse maintains an important population of beneficial bacteria in the hind-gut. These bacteria break down the otherwise-indigestible cellulose; the horse absorbs the valuable by-products of this digestion (the VFAs) through the gut walls. Because the hind-gut is located *after* the small intestine in the GI tract, enzymes are no longer directly digesting the gut content, including bacteria. Therefore, bacteria pass intact from the hind-gut through the feces. It's the by-products of the bacterial digestion that the horse absorbs and uses. The horse is in effect in symbiosis with the bacteria, which survive on the cellulose that the horse couldn't otherwise digest.

Anything that damages the bacteria will upset this vital balance. This can include drugs like wormers, NSAIDS, and oral antibiotics. Sudden changes in food supply can also overwhelm the good bacteria. Dehydration of the gut or an increase in body temperature, as with a fever, can also kill the bacteria and cause problems.

Wormers Explained
Wormers are drugs that are carefully selected to cause minimal harm to the gut bacteria. Basically, all wormers are neurotoxins, and because bacteria don't have nervous systems, they are not generally affected. Worms, being multi-cellular organisms, do have a basic nervous system and are the target of these drugs. However, wormers given in excessive doses can harm the beneficial bacteria. So correct dosage is important.

usually high in fiber and indigestible portions, are passed on into the cecum and colons. This next section of the GI tract is the portion usually referred to as the "hind-gut."

Cecum

The cecum, the first of the three large fermentation sacs, is a blind-ended sac containing a large population of microbes. It is in here that the bacterial degradation of cellulose begins. This bacterial degradation, or fermentation, produces as a by-product the Volatile Fatty Acids (VFAs) acetate, butyrate, and propionate. VFAs are in fact simple fats and enter the metabolism of the body as a source of

Unfriendly Bacteria
A range of species of bacteria is present in the GI tract; not all of them beneficial. Some are actually pathogens that can cause disease, but as long as the beneficial bacteria are flourishing, they keep the numbers of pathogenic organisms in check. If the balance gets upset, however, the pathogens can gain the upper hand. If the beneficial bacteria die in large numbers, they provide food for the pathogens. As they die, they release toxins into the colons. These toxins are absorbed by the colon walls and can lead to a general toxemia, most often resulting in the horse foundering. Thus it is important not to upset the gut bacteria — they need to be kept happy and healthy.

Feeding the Good Guys
Probiotics are a means of supplying beneficial bacteria in the form of an inoculant, or a dose of dried bacteria, to the gut, the intention being to resupply so-called "good bugs." Probiotics don't need to be fed every day; in fact, they should only be necessary from time to time, say following worming, or if drugs are being given orally, or if the horse overheats.

There are other products that "feed" the beneficial bugs and help them to grow. One option is Diamond V Yeast. The yeast is food for the bacteria; thus these products should be fed on a daily basis.

Feeds that are high in soluble fiber help beneficial bacteria thrive. However, concentrates cause them to grow too quickly, leading to problems with overgrowth, and too much of a good thing is not good. The health of the hind-gut is all about balance!

fat. These VFAs are absorbed by the walls of the cecum and are transported to the liver, where they enter into the overall energy metabolism of the body, especially fat metabolism. VFAs are valuable sources of energy to the horse. (See Chapter 2.) It should be noted that VFAs, being fats, are not involved in the glycemic response. (See sidebar, pages 12–13.)

Colons

There are two colons, called the dorsal and the ventral colon. These huge sacs contain populations of bacteria that continue the process of bacterial fermentation that begins in the cecum. The walls of the colons are able to absorb VFAs and water-soluble vitamins. The two large sacs are joined by a very small, narrow transverse colon. The combination of large sacs joined by a small narrow pipe tends to predispose the horse to blockages called, in common parlance, impaction colics. This physical peculiarity of the hind-gut will figure prominently in the discussion of colic and its causes in Chapter 8.

Small Colon and Rectum

The small colon and rectum are the site for absorption of 90 percent of the water from digesta, which is very important for the water balance of the body. The rectum walls form the fecal balls and collect the material prior to expulsion.

The Gastrointestinal (GI) Tract

The GI tract is suspended from the wall of the peritoneum by a membrane called the mesentery. This membrane, which is very thin, is subject to tearing and twisting. If it tears, then portions of gut become unsupported, free to swing, rotate, and twist. This can result in a twisted gut. If a colicking horse rolls because of the pain from a blockage or impaction, causing a section of the gut to twist, a far greater problem than the original impaction results. A twisted gut is a very serious condition, usually fatal, and can be resolved only by surgery. Always do your best to keep a colicky horse from rolling to minimize this risk. (For more information on colic, see Chapter 8.)

The gastrointestinal tract plays an important role, digestively speaking. The absorbed nutrients — sugars, proteins, vitamins, minerals (but not the fats) — are collected in the blood vessels that perfuse through the GI tract walls. All of these small vessels collect into the hepatic portal vein, which conveys absorbed nutrients to the liver. All the components of blood — the cells, plus the liquid portion of the blood carrying the dissolved nutrients — are conveyed to the liver for processing.

In the liver, any absorbed toxins are detoxified, the amino acids are sorted and re-formed into proteins, and the water-soluble vitamins and minerals are bound to their respective carriers. Some go into storage and some into use, depending on the animal's needs at any given moment and the content of the meal. The only exception is fat, which is absorbed from the small intestine by the lymph and enters the circulation in the lymph nodes of the neck. Thus, the fat from the meal finds its way to the liver after it has already circulated around the body. The fact that fat is absorbed by a different route than other nutrients is key to understanding equine nutrition and the significance of fat-soluble nutrients — and fat-soluble toxins.

BASIC FACTS OF FEEDING

- The horse essentially needs to be fed fiber (i.e., hay or grass) with extra calories from fat or starch added only as required to meet his caloric or nutritional needs (discussed in Chapter 2).
- Horses are trickle feeders and cannot digestively cope with large meals. "Little and often" is the rule.
- The horse exists in symbiosis with his gut bacteria, which must be kept healthy. Avoid sudden changes in feed type, and always provide plenty of fiber to nourish the beneficial gut flora. Minimize the use of oral drugs whenever possible.
- Horses digest the soluble portion of their food directly, and then access the energy in the fiber via bacterial fermentation.

-2-

All About Nutrients

IN A NUTSHELL, A NUTRIENT IS ANY FEED CONSTITUENT that is necessary for the support of life. Nutrients accomplish this life support function by providing fundamental components of body structure, or by enhancing or enabling chemical processes that occur in the body, like metabolism. They can also provide transportation for other nutrients into, through, or out of the body. Nutrients can assist with metabolic control, and they may be substances that affect feed palatability and digestion and thus influence intake and availability.

There are six basic classes of nutrients: water, proteins, fats, carbohydrates, minerals, and vitamins. It is helpful to understand what each of these nutrients does and how they are supplied in the feed and handled by the body. It helps to think of feed as nutrient packages, each kind supplying a different mix of nutrients; the overall goal of feeding is to supply a balance of nutrients in the various packages. This balance should match as closely as possible the requirements of the horse at its particular stage of life. With the exception of specific vitamin and mineral supplements, most feeds usually contain a mix of nutrients that crosses the entire spectrum, although they differ in the relative amounts they supply. For example, hay, corn, oats, and soybean meal all contain a mix of all the nutrients, but corn and oats also contain a much higher amount of carbohydrates than hay, and soybean meal will contain a higher level of protein than any of the others. Correct feeding is the art and science of blending the various ingredients to produce a balanced whole.

Water

Water is the most essential nutrient of all. Every life process that occurs on a cellular level and within the organs of the body, including digestion, takes place in a solution of water. Water also supplies essential hydrogen and oxygen atoms. A horse can live for weeks without food but only for a few days without water.

When more water is lost — through eliminating solid and liquid waste, sweating, and even breathing — than the horse can replace by drinking, dehydration results. Dehydration can lead to problems of varying seriousness, from colic and interference with normal cell functions (such as an inability to use muscles), to collapse of the kidneys. Therefore, horses should constantly have available a reliable source of clean, fresh drinking water.

The best way to ensure sufficient water is to supply it free choice and allow the horse to drink his fill.

Voluntary water intake for a horse at rest on a cool day is considered to be adequate at around half a gallon per 100 pounds bodyweight. As a rule of thumb, the water requirement for maintenance, in gallons, is considered the same as the energy requirement in Megacalories (see Appendix). So a horse that needs 3.3 Mcal/day for maintenance should consume 3.3 gallons of water. Water requirements increase with temperature and work. The requirement on a hot day or when exercising will be considerably more than the maintenance requirement, up to three or four times as much.

The best way to ensure sufficient water is to supply it free choice and allow the horse to drink his fill. If clean water at a reasonable temperature is supplied, horses will generally drink sufficient amounts for their needs. However, if the water is poor quality (tastes bad) or the temperature is very low or very high, they may not consume enough and may suffer from dehydration.

Water intake requirements also increase with the amount of dry matter in the feed. Thus horses consuming a diet of hay and grain will drink more than horses grazing on fresh grass in the pasture.

Insufficient water intake is very detrimental. The first signs of dehydration are reduced dry matter feed intake, followed by reduced physical activity and impairment of ability. There is an increased risk of colic and a reduction in body weight. The physical signs, such as dry mouth and sunken eyes, occur once there has been a 6 percent or more loss of body weight. Impairment of physical ability occurs at about half of this level of weight loss, around 3 percent of body weight. As the dehydration progresses, output of

QUALITY COUNTS

Naturally, water intake is reduced when water is unpalatable or inaccessible. Dissolved salts can make water taste bad (see next page). In winter, a water trough with an electric heater that has a wiring problem will shock the animal each time it tries to drink. If the water is frozen, horses will eat a small amount of snow, but intake will be insufficient to meet needs. In winter, therefore, it is important to ensure that there is liquid water available and to encourage adequate intake by warming it, if possible.

fluid in the urine is reduced, and urine becomes stronger smelling, more viscous, and darker in color.

Water Quality

The single most reliable indicator of water quality is Total Dissolved Salts, or TDS, also called salinity. For livestock, it should be below 5,000 ppm (parts per million); non-pregnant or non-lactating horses can safely consume water with a TDS of 7,000 ppm, but it will tend to have a strong taste and they may well reject it until they are used to it. Testing the water for TDS can be done by any water testing lab; look in the commercial pages of your phone book.

TDS should not be confused with "hardness," which is not a direct measure of total salts, but a measure of the tendency of the water to form a scum with soaps. The salts that cause hardness are usually salts of magnesium or calcium but can include iron and zinc as well. Hardness is not usually a problem in terms of drinking water, because the magnesium salts are tasteless and horses readily drink hard water. The contribution of the dissolved magnesium salts to the overall mineral requirements of the horse is not known at this time, but since it is almost impossible to overdose magnesium by mouth (the GI tract absorbs only what the horse needs, the rest is excreted), there are no real concerns over hard water safety.

Water quality may be adversely affected, however, by toxins such as pesticides, heavy metals and other chemical pollutants, fertilizer run-off, toxic bacteria, and algae. Fertilizer and pesticide run-off tends to be a concern with ponds that drain from fertilized fields. Water that drains from livestock pens or yards is often contaminated with bacteria and can spread disease. The bacteria of most concern are salmonella and fecal coliforms.

Ponds and Streams

Because some forms of blue-green algae that grow on pond water can cause toxicity, do not allow horses to drink from affected ponds. This algae contamination frequently occurs in water that contains a high level of organic material, such as those near slurry pits or fields that have been fertilized. Thus, ponds and stagnant water are not good sources of drinking water for horses. Water in streams might have pollution sources upstream and can be very variable in quality. The safest water sources are public utility water or a well that has passed inspection.

SOME WATER SOLUTIONS

• Horses don't readily drink very cold water and will consume less than optimal amounts if their water is too cold. Most of the year this is not an issue, but in winter the horse is more likely to consume adequate amounts of water if it is warmed or heated.

• High levels of minerals are not necessarily unhealthy but may contribute a strong flavor, and most horses will reject such water if they are not accustomed to it. This can be a problem if you are shipping them long distances, for example, to show grounds. One solution is to haul some water from home for them to drink initially, but this is not always practical, especially if you'll be away for an extended time. Another strategy is to add a strong flavoring such as Kool-Aid that overcomes the alien taste. Get horses used to the flavoring at home and then add it when you get to your destination as well, so the water tastes and smells familiar.

• If there are leaves or vegetation in your water source, the tannic acid they contain can cause the water to taste bitter and hence put the horses off drinking it. Field troughs located under trees are particularly prone to this. In sufficient quantity, tannic acid is toxic, so don't allow the leaves to accumulate. In general, keep pasture troughs as clean as possible.

• Keep troughs clean by emptying, scrubbing out, and refilling on a monthly or bi-monthly basis, and if you can, position them away from trees. If you find algae, after cleaning, use about 25cc of bleach per 25 gallons of water when you rinse out the trough to delay algae regrowth.

• If you have a system that continually allows water to flow into a trough and out via a drain, you can maintain a population of goldfish or small catfish in the trough to eat the algae. Make sure that water levels are adequate at all times for the fish to survive and that the water is oxygenated by allowing it to flow. Do not add bleach to troughs inhabited by fish. The fish trough-cleaning plan is best for troughs that are close to the barn and can be checked at regular intervals.

Testing Water

If your horse's drinking water supply is in a vulnerable location (pond water, for example, or downhill from a manure pit or fertilized field), it might be advisable to have your water tested. If the horses show signs of dehydration or refuse to drink enough, then definitely test the water.

If you are using water from a public utility or a well that has passed inspection, then just make sure any heated stock tanks are not shocking the horses. Test by sticking your hand in the water!

Energy

Energy is not in itself a nutrient; it has no mass or dimension. Energy, however, is essential for all cellular functions. The cells use energy for all activities, such as transmitting nervous impulses, contracting muscles, making other molecules, building membranes, making new cells, pumping ions, and digesting food. Within the cell, energy is derived from the oxidation (combining with oxygen) of the chemical bonds of molecules, generating molecules of Adenosine Tri-Phosphate (ATP), the "energy currency" of the cell. All the biochemical processes require energy, which is shuttled around the cell and passed from one area to another via the molecules of ATP.

In the body, energy can be converted to heat. The heat can be measured, and this measurement provides an indirect analysis of the energy content of a feed. In physics the amount of energy/heat needed to raise the temperature of one gram of water by one degree centigrade is the small calorie. In nutrition, we generally use the large Calorie, also called a Kilocalorie (Kcal, or 1,000 calories), which is the heat required to raise one kilogram of water by one degree. In large animals like horses we usually specify Megacalories (Mcal). One Mcal has the same energy as 1,000 Kcal. If you know your horse's bodyweight in pounds, divide by 100. Multiply that number by 1.5 to derive the Mcals your horse needs for maintenance.

When a food is burned in a bomb calorimeter and the resulting heat measured, that heat measurement provides the Gross Energy, or GE, of the feed. In the animal's digestive tract, however, some parts of the food are too resistant to digestion to be broken down, and the undigested portions are passed out in the feces. To arrive at the Digestible Energy, or DE, of feed, the difference between the GE of the feed and the GE of the feces is compared; the difference represents the energy the horse actually received through digestion. When we talk about the energy value of a feed we usually mean the Digestible Energy.

Energy is derived from feed primarily from the oxidation of two nutrients: fats and carbohydrates. Proteins can be used to provide energy, especially in emergencies, but it is wasteful and sometimes harmful to continually feed protein as an energy source. It can result in unpleasant side effects, such as excess urine production and high ammonia output. Excess urine output can strain the kidneys. At the least, overfeeding protein is a waste of money.

Sometimes on a feed label, you will notice the term "TDN" in reference to the energy value. TDN stands for Total Digestible Nutrients and is a measure of the digestible energy — carbohydrates, proteins, and fat — given as weight or percent. (The fat value is multiplied by 2.25, because fat contains 2.25 times as much energy per pound as carbohydrates and proteins do.) One pound TDN = 2.0 Mcal (or 1kg TDN = 4.4 Mcal). (For more details on how to calculate the energy and feed requirements, refer to Chapter 4.) Since some feed companies use TDN and some use Mcals, this information will help you translate between the two. All ration formulation in this book will be in Mcal.

Striking a Balance

When balancing a ration for horses, it is important to meet the energy needs first before considering the other requirements. For maintenance, a mature non-working, non-pregnant, non-lactating horse requires roughly 1.5 Mcal per 100 pounds of bodyweight per day. To meet the additional requirements of work, pregnancy, lactation, or growth, additional calories must be supplied (see Appendix table 4 for energy requirements). If the horse consumes less energy than he needs, he will lose body weight, mostly from fat stores, but also from muscle. If the horse consumes more energy than he

Heavier horses need more fuel than light ones do.

needs, he will store the excess as fat and you end up with a fat horse. To determine if your horse is under or overweight, use the Body Score Scale (see Chapter 5). Ideally, most horses should score around a 5 or a 6 on this assessment scale.

The bulk of the horse's energy requirements fuel basic maintenance. In a pregnant mare, 50 percent of her energy requirement is for her own maintenance, with the balance used to provide energy to the fetus. In young, growing horses, 60–95 percent is required for maintenance, leaving between 5–40 percent available for growth. The requirement for maintenance is based on bodyweight — heavier horses need more fuel than light ones do. When the energy needs in mature, non-pregnant horses are calculated, after bodyweight, the most important consideration for energy requirements is workload. Workload is divided into light, moderate, and heavy duty, depending on the speed, duration, and weight carried or pulled. See Chapter 4 and Chapter 5 for more about determining your horse's specific energy requirements.

Carbohydrates

As the name implies, carbohydrates (CHO) are molecules that consist of carbon, hydrogen, and oxygen. All carbohydrates are variations of the ring molecules called sugars. Sugars consist of either five or six carbon atoms arranged in a ring, with oxygen and hydrogen atoms attached. The simplest sugar of all is the 5-carbon glucose. (The term -ose means sugar: for example, glucose, mannose, lactose, etc.) Glucose is the sugar that all cells can use for energy and is the fuel of choice for many cells.

Carbohydrates consist of chains of sugars joined together. They are usually divided into two types. Short, simple chains of sugars that are soluble in water are called non-structural carbohydrates; they are usually in solution in the cell itself. Longer, more complex chains of sugars are called structural carbohydrates. These are the complex molecules that make up the cell walls of plants and contribute rigidity to wood. Examples are cellulose, hemi-cellulose and lignin.

ALL ABOUT NON-STRUCTURAL CARBOHYDRATES, CELLULOSE, AND LIGNINS

Carbohydrates are complex molecules that combine carbon, hydrogen, and oxygen atoms — hence the name. The simplest carbohydrate is the sugar molecule. When plants photosynthesize, they use the energy of sunlight to convert water and carbon dioxide into simple sugars, such as fructose and glucose. These simple sugars are then bound together to form the more complex disaccharides, such as sucrose or mannose. The disaccharides can then later become chains that form the more complex starch molecules.

Plants store carbohydrates as starch. The plant uses some of the starch and sugar it makes to produce its main cell wall and structural components. Within cell walls, the chains of sugar molecules are not just straight, but also branch and interlink to form the stronger substance, cellulose. If the cell walls are in the stem or main support of the plant, the cellulose is further strengthened by binding in nitrogen atoms to produce lignin, a very hard, strong, woody substance.

Starch and sugar are the Non-Structural Carbohydrates (NSC), or simple carbs, and cellulose and lignin are the complex carbs. The ease of digestion is related to the degree of complexity of the binding and cross-linking within the plant's structure. Simple carbs form bonds that are easy to break and quickly digested in the gastrointestinal (GI) tract of horses, while the complex carb cellulose, with its stronger cellular bonds, needs help from bacteria to be broken down. Lignin is indigestible, even to bacteria.

In the GI tract of the horse, the non-structural carbohydrates are broken down to simple sugars, such as fructose or glucose, and are absorbed. The sugars then pass to the liver, which sorts them and converts most of them to the simple sugar glucose. The glucose is released from the liver and travels to all cells of the body. Under the influence of the hormone insulin, the cells withdraw the glucose from the bloodstream and utilize it for energy. If there is more glucose coming in from the bloodstream than the cell needs, it stores the extra glucose as the compound glycogen. If excess glucose continues to be supplied, then the adipocytes (special fat producing cells) absorb it and convert it to fat and store it.

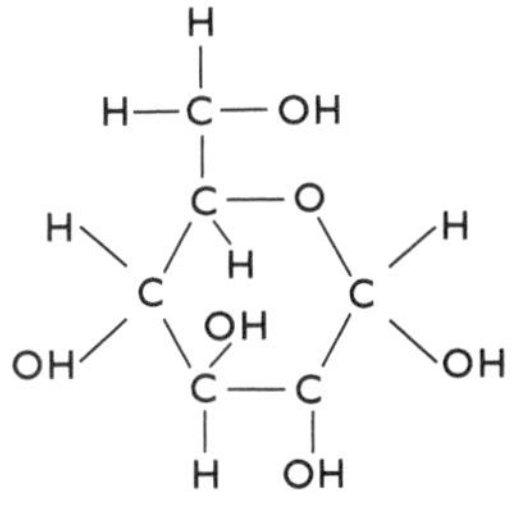

Sugar molecule

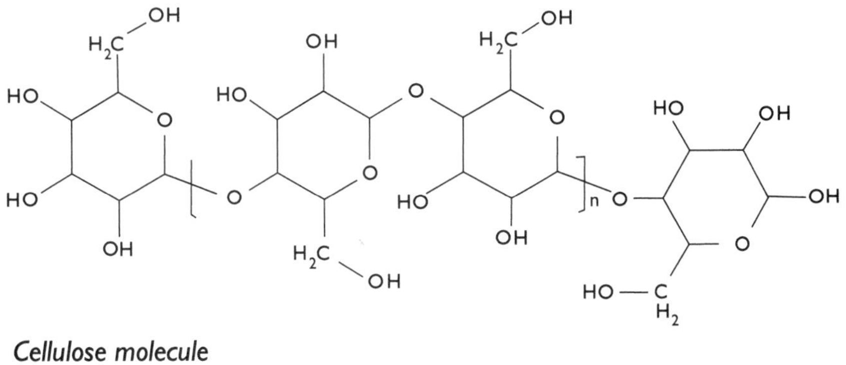

Cellulose molecule

Most cells of the body can use the incoming glucose or the stored fat as an energy source, with the choice of energy source depending on which is most readily available. But some cells, namely kidney medulla and red blood cells, can *only* use glucose and must have a supply of it if they are to function. The nerve cells of the brain can adapt to using fat if they are forced to by persistently low blood sugar, but the kidney and red blood cells must utilize glucose from carbohydrates.

Starches and sugars, the simple carbohydrates, are digested in the small intestine by all mammals, including the horse. These simple carbohydrates, the Non-Structural Carbohydrates or NSC fraction, are sometimes called Non-Fiber Carbohydrates (NFC). In the small intestine, they are broken down to the component sugars, which cross the GI tract wall and proceed to the liver. If the level of glucose in the blood goes up (as it does during the digestion process), the blood sugar level rises. The rising blood sugar triggers the release of the hormone insulin from the pancreas. This insulin is necessary for muscle cells and other body cells to absorb the glucose from the bloodstream.

The more complex molecules, such as cellulose, contain special branching linkages called beta-glycan links. As we learned in Chapter 1, mammals do not possess the enzymes to break these links; only bacteria do. This is why large mammals that eat a lot of grass depend on bacteria to help them digest. Herbivores all possess sizable fermentation tanks (rumen or cecum and colons) where the cell wall material can be mixed with bacteria so the bacteria can break it down in the process known as bacterial fermentation.

In the process of breaking down cell walls, the bacteria excrete waste products. Some of these waste products are simple short-chain fatty acids (VFAs, short for volatile fatty acids). These fatty acids are absorbed from the cecum and colons and pass to the liver, where they are used in energy production. One of the VFAs, called propionate, can be used by the liver to make glucose molecules; thus, while the other two fats, acetate and butyrate, go into fat metabolism, the propionate can be processed for carbohydrate metabolism.

Horses that consume a low glycemic diet — primarily fiber — can obtain the glucose they need from the propionate produced by bacteria in their cecum and colons. Because the fats acetate and butyrate do not raise the blood sugar, and it takes the propionate a long time to convert to glucose, digesting fiber does not elevate the horse's blood sugar levels, nor does it trigger insulin release. This factor is important to understand in cases of insulin resistance, founder, and metabolic bone disease, discussed in Chapter 8.

Fats

Fats are the richest energy sources. As we saw earlier, an ounce of fat will yield 2.25 times more energy than an ounce of carbohydrate.

Referred to as lipids, or fatty acids, this class of nutrients includes volatile fatty acids (VFAs), produced by bacteria in the hind-gut. Horses can digest dietary fat, such as the fats in oil seeds like whole roast soy, flax, or safflower or corn oil; their liver produces bile salts to facilitate this type of fat digestion. Up to 10 percent of the diet can be supplied as fat, especially if the horse has a higher energy

NOT ALL FATS ARE CREATED EQUAL!

There is more to understand about fat than its role in providing an energy supply.

Fats (aka lipids) are chains of carbon atoms with hydrogen and oxygen branching out to the side. The chains vary in length from very simple two-carbon acetate up to chains of 30 or more carbon atoms. Most of the atoms in the chains are held to the adjacent carbon atoms by single bonds; these are called saturated fats. However, some fats have double bonds between two adjacent carbon atoms, and these are referred to as unsaturated fats. A few of them have more than one double bond. These are called polyunsaturated fats.

Horses (and other mammals) can manufacture fats from excess carbohydrate, fat, and protein molecules, but they can produce only the single bonds, so all the fats the horse makes are saturated. Polyunsaturated fats, however, are necessary in many functions. There are places where the body requires double bonds in the lipid molecules, but since it cannot manufacture these double bonds, the fats in question must be supplied in the diet.

Polyunsaturated fats make up a special subgroup of fats, called Essential Fatty Acids, or EFAs. The most important EFAs are linolenic, arachidonic, and linoleic acids; these are called the Omega-3 and Omega-6 fatty acids. They are found in certain plants, such as flax and other oilseeds, and in some cold-water fish, such as salmon and cod. Their availability in plant products and fish oils depends on the oils and fats remaining unprocessed by heat or by chemical means.

If fat is oxidized, it becomes chemically altered, which we refer to as going rancid. To increase shelf life and slow the rate of oxidation, fats in foods are processed by partial or complete hydrogenation. Because polyunsaturated fats are fragile and easily damaged by exposure to heat, light, and oxygen (air), the preservation process tends to destroy the unsaturated bonds, which means that the oil no longer contains EFAs.

need than can be supplied by grasses or grains. However, not all fats are created equal. (See sidebar, previous page.)

Feeding Balanced EFAs

The body uses the EFAs to produce hormones called prostaglandins (PGs). These are a class of compound used extensively as chemical messengers within the body. The EFAs are classified into one of three families, depending on which kind of prostaglandin they can produce. PG-1s are produced from a family of EFAs found in the oils of safflower, corn, sunflower, peanut, and evening primrose. PG-2s are derived from Omega-6 fatty acids found in animal products, such as meat and dairy products, mollusks, and shellfish. PG-3s are derived from the Omega-3 fatty acids found in highest concentrations in walnut, olive, canola, linseed (flaxseed), hemp, and cold-water fish oils. The body needs all three types of EFAs to produce the various PGs it needs.

Prostaglandin PG-2 is a compound important in development of pain signals and in signaling inflammatory responses. The other two kinds of prostaglandins, PGs 1 and 3, appear to play important roles in tissue repair, growth regulation, central nervous system activity, and the modulation of inflammation. The amount of each prostaglandin produced depends on the relative concentration of each family of EFA in the diet. Partial or complete hydrogenation of the fats results in a higher level of production of PG-2. Higher levels of PG-2 may result in increased rates of degenerative diseases and an increased perception of pain. Increasing the levels of PGs 1 and 3 has, in human nutrition, been shown to decrease pain perception and to decrease the rate of degenerative disease development.

So how to increase the level of the beneficial Omega-3 fatty acids in the horse's diet? One way to raise the relative levels in the diet is to feed flaxseed, canola, or walnut oil, but these oils are fairly expensive. To ensure that there has been no loss of EFAs, they must be cold-pressed, in a dark, oxygen-free environment. EFAs degenerate quickly upon exposure to light and air. Flaxseed oil, for example, must be kept in dark, closed containers and refrigerated. While fresh canola oil has a reasonably high level of EFAs, commercially available canola oil is processed, and the EFAs will have been lost.

A better method is to feed whole linseed, or flaxseed, because it contains the highest levels of Omega-3 fatty acids. It used to be advised to grind or soak the seeds first but this not really necessary; just add 1 cupful per day of the whole, dry seed.

The old-fashioned way to feed flax to horses was to cook it, usually for hours. This opened the seed coat and removed any possibility of toxicity due to the cyanogenic glycosides that were present in the seed coat of the old varieties. Unfortunately, extensive cooking destroys all the Omega-3 fatty acids, although all the other good nutrients (the protein fraction and the other fats) remained, so it was still a valuable feed. However, modern cultivars of flaxseed no longer contain glycoside and hence are safe if fed whole. You can grind or soak the seeds for 20 minutes prior to feeding, but this is not really necessary.

The addition of two to four ounces of whole flaxseed to a horse's diet daily or every other day will make a tremendous contribution to improved skin and coat condition, hoof growth, rate of healing from injury, and arthritic conditions. Plus, as a welcome bonus, the seeds are high in mucilage, which is a wonderful GI tract lubricant and is very useful in preventing impactions and colic.

If using whole flaxseed is not feasible, there are a number of commercial products available that contain flaxseed. Some companies also offer canine and human versions.

Producing Energy for Muscles

One of the current hot topics of discussion among horsefolk centers on reducing the quantity of carbohydrates and increasing levels of fat when feeding performance horses. What is the difference between supplying energy from carbohydrates versus fat? It all boils down to the cellular processes of generating energy within the muscle.

For a muscle to generate the powerful thrust necessary to propel a horse, it must contract. This means that the individual fibers must shorten in length, achieved when muscle filaments slide over one another. The energy for that contraction comes from Adenosine Triphosphate, or ATP, produced within muscle cells. The expended ATP must be regenerated within the muscle cells by one of two pathways. (A pathway is a series of biochemical steps or reactions controlled by enzymes.)

One energy-producing pathway does not require oxygen (anaerobic) and takes place in the cell cytoplasm. The other pathway requires oxygen (aerobic) and occurs in organelles within the cell called mitochondria, which provide the bulk of the power supply for the cell.

The aerobic pathway for ATP regeneration, known as oxidative phosphorylation (also the citric acid cycle or the Krebs cycle), occurs in the mitochondria. It is very efficient in terms of the number of ATP molecules generated (11 molecules of ATP per glucose molecule). However, this process can only generate ATP in the presence of sufficient oxygen. When glucose from carbohydrates is used for energy, there is a pathway in the cellular cytoplasm that first splits each glucose molecule into two pyruvate molecules (releasing two ATP molecules for each glucose molecule). These pyruvate molecules enter the mitochondria and proceed into oxidative phosphorylation. The end products of oxidative phosphorylation are carbon dioxide, water, and ATPs.

When a cell requires energy under conditions when insufficient oxygen is available for the mitochondria to work, anaerobic metabolism takes place in a process known as glycolysis. The anaerobic pathway is fast, but it produces a limited amount of ATP per glucose molecule. The only fuel that the anaerobic pathway can use is glucose.

If glycolysis continues while the mitochondria are shut down for lack of oxygen, pyruvate accumulates and begins to block the process. To allow the pathway to continue processing glucose and generating ATP, the pyruvate must be removed. It cannot enter the mitochondria because they have been turned off due to lack of oxygen. So the cell resorts to another method of removal, converting pyruvate to lactate to clear the blockage, which then allows more pyruvate to be generated, producing additional ATP.

However, lactate is very damaging to the cell. The accumulation of lactate in the bloodstream is sometimes referred to as "oxygen debt" or the anaerobic threshold. Because the muscle cell does not possess the enzymes to reconvert the lactate to pyruvate and glucose, lactate is diffused out of the cell into the bloodstream, which transports it to the liver, where it can be recycled by enzymes into pyruvate and glucose.

By this pathway, the cell is able to generate ATPs for muscle power even when oxygen is insufficient, though that comes at a price: inefficiency and the accumulation of cell-damaging lactate.

The Role of Fats

Glucose can be converted to energy in both pathways, but fats can be utilized only in the aerobic pathway. Why is this?

Within the muscle cell, fat molecules, which are long chains of hydrocarbon molecules, are split to yield two hydrocarbon units, known as acetyl units. These hydrocarbon units are joined to a molecule called Coenzyme-A (usually abbreviated to Co-A) to form another molecule called acetyl Co-A. When the acetyl Co-A is made, five ATPs are formed. The acetyl Co-A enters the mitochondria. Once in the mitochondria, each acetyl Co-A goes through oxidative phosphorylation to yield 12 ATP molecules. Thus, as it proceeds through oxidation, a fat with 16 hydrocarbons in its chain can yield 129 molecules of ATP. Fats can supply lots of ATP, but only in the mitochondria through aerobic metabolism.

When muscles are contracting quickly (such as for running or jumping), there is no time to supply sufficient oxygen to the mitochondria, and the pathway is suddenly unable to supply enough ATP. When the horse jumps or accelerates hard, the sudden thrust requires a certain amount of power or energy. Because insufficient amounts of oxygen are supplied to allow aerobic metabolism to meet the demand for power, the cell makes ATP available through anaerobic metabolism, allowing the muscle to contract forcefully and complete the action. After the need for power has passed, the cell can return to the more efficient process of aerobic metabolism.

Under normal aerobic circumstances, cells prefer to oxidize fats because they are more energy-efficient, but under conditions of low oxygen this pathway is unavailable. In order to continue to supply ATP for the muscle to contract, cells switch to the glycolic pathway, which is able to operate without oxygen.

Certain muscle cells are better set up to oxidize fat, while others are better set up to use glycolysis. The muscle cells that prefer glycolysis are designated as fast twitch, low oxidative (requiring low oxygen), or Type A fibers. The muscle cells that are better set up to use oxidative metabolism are called slow twitch, or high oxidative, Type B fibers. Training influences the relative development of these fibers. Thus, training a horse with short bursts of fast, explosive work (sprinting or jumping) develops the fast twitch fibers. Slow, long distance work will develop the slow twitch fibers. The fuel the horse is fed will also help to develop the right fibers. Horses that primarily do a lot of fast, explosive work must have some of their energy provided as fat but most of it as carbohydrates (which produce glucose). Horses that do slow, steady work need some of their energy as carbs but can better utilize fats.

Thus the fuel a cell uses depends on oxygen supply. Under aerobic conditions (slow work), a cell will oxidize fat. As the speed of contraction increases, however, the supply of oxygen becomes insufficient and cells switch to glycolysis, using glucose from carbohydrates as their fuel.

An adequate supply of glucose is essential for working muscle cells. Glucose is stored within the cell as the compound glycogen. As the workload of the cell increases, the use of glycogen also increases to maintain the vital supply of ATP. When the cell exhausts its supply of stored glycogen, it will stop contracting, even if sufficient fat and oxygen are being supplied. Therefore, supplying as much of the needed fuel as possible in the form of fat can extend glycogen supplies and allow the cell to continue its work for longer. This is why supplying some of the horse's energy as fat is beneficial.

Furthermore, fats are not only valuable as an energy source. They are also essential components of cell membranes and provide building blocks for important enzymes. So every horse needs a certain amount of fat in its diet, even if it is not using it for energy.

Protein Basics

Protein is the main structural component of body, consisting of chains of amino acids. All enzymes are proteins, as well as most of the cell matrix. Yet except in the skeletal muscle, there is no body store of protein. The quality of a protein source is defined by how well the range of amino acids it supplies matches the requirements of the animal.

There are twenty-two amino acids that comprise all the proteins the body makes and uses. The liver can synthesize twelve of these; the other ten cannot be synthesized and must be supplied in the diet. These ten are called essential amino acids.

ESSENTIAL AMINO ACIDS

NAME	ABBREVIATION
Arginine	Arg
Histidine	His
Isoleucine	Iso
Leucine	Leu
Lysine	Lys
Methionine	Met
Phenylalanine	Phe
Threonine	Tre
Tryptophan	Trp
Valine	Val

NONESSENTIAL AMINO ACIDS

NAME	ABBREVIATION
Alanine	Ala
Asparagine	Asn
Aspartate	Asp
Cysteine	Cys (is non-essential if enough Met is present)
Glutamate	Glu
Glutamine	Gla
Glycine	Gly
Hydroxyproline	Hyp
Hydroylysine	Hyd
Proline	Pro
Serine	Ser
Tyrosine	Tyr

Compare a protein to a sentence: words are made up of letters that must be present in the right order for it to make sense. Not all twenty-six letters are needed all the time, but certain letters are needed much more often than others. If any letters needed to complete a word are missing, the sentence remains unfinished until the correct letter is provided.

When the body digests incoming protein, it is first broken down into its component amino acids (the letters). The amino acids are absorbed and channeled to the liver, where they are sorted. The liver releases the amino acids to the tissues, where they are utilized in forming new proteins in the cells (the words).

Proteins are synthesized by cell organelles called ribosomes. The ribosome works along adding the next amino acid to the chain as instructed by the m-RNA (messenger RNA). If instructed to add a certain amino acid — for example, lysine — and if no lysine is available because not enough has been supplied in the diet, then protein production ceases until the needed amino acid arrives. It does not matter how much of the other amino acids are available. If the required one is missing, then the production of that protein is halted. The sentence can't be completed.

When missing amino acids impede protein production, particularly if the protein being made is a particularly important one, there is potential for a real problem. For example, if keratin, the main protein of hoof and hair, is being produced and there is insufficient methionine available, then keratin production is slowed or even halted until it becomes available again.

The quality of a protein is a measure of how many of the essential amino acids the protein contains and, more importantly, how closely the balance of the essential amino acids matches the requirements of the animal. The protein needs to supply enough of the essential amino acids to allow protein synthesis to proceed; if the protein supplies a lot of amino acids that are already present and none of the needed ones, the "sentence" remains incomplete.

Protein quality is rarely assessed for horse feeds, yet it can be a real factor in how well the animal uses the proteins supplied in the feed. Unfortunately, the amino acid make-up is rarely included in the information supplied by the feed manufacturer. The best way to get this information is to contact the manufacturer and ask for an amino acid profile for the feed in question. In field crops, profiles are rarely supplied or used. The easiest solution for a horse owner who suspects his or her protein quality may not be adequate is to supplement the diet with a good quality essential amino acid source. There are a number of commercial mixes available.

Feeding Adequate Protein

The protein value provided on a feed label can be more than a bit misleading. Most times the feed value is given just as a percentage or an amount, with no mention of quality; furthermore, the amount stated on the bag is usually given as crude protein rather than digestible protein.

The feed value crude protein listed on the bag label is not really a measure of the protein per se, but an indirect guesstimate. The way it is calculated is by measuring the nitrogen content of the feed. An assumption is made that because protein contains 16 percent nitrogen, you can calculate the "protein" from the amount of nitrogen the feed contains. Hence the term crude protein. This is fine as long as all the nitrogen present is in the protein; however, it does not make an allowance for the nitrogen contained in the non-protein fractions. As a result, the crude protein value you read on the bag tends to be an overestimate of the actual protein content.

Then there is the question of protein quality. As we've seen, the quality of a protein is a measure of how many of the essential amino acids are supplied by the particular protein. The quality is more important than the absolute quantity. If the essential amino acids are not present, then the protein present is not bio-available and will be excreted in the urine. You can see this effect when you feed a low-quality protein source like alfalfa; the horse's urine output increases, and the high levels of nitrogen that the urine contains make it very strong smelling. However, adding methionine, lysine, or threonine to a low-quality protein such as alfalfa can reduce urine output, because the essential amino acids enable the horse to utilize more of the protein.

Any shortage of essential amino acids will create the same symptoms as general protein shortage. Feeding good-quality proteins from several different sources is the best way to ensure a mix of amino acids. Also, a good-quality protein can be fed in smaller amounts and causes far less stress on the liver and kidneys. This is preferable to feeding a lot of low-quality protein. Low-quality protein can be made more useful by the addition of the essential amino acids they are lowest in. In horse diets, this usually means addition of lysine, methionine, and threonine.

In general, most individual amino acids don't actually have separate functions except as components of proteins, and the symptoms of any shortfall are evident as general protein deficiency symptoms. Many times, the only way to know if you are feeding a low-quality protein is from the amount of urine that your horse produces.

If you are feeding too much protein that can't be processed by the horse's body, urine output will be high, leaving a strong smell of ammonia. This is a reliable indicator of a diet that is low in essential amino acids.

Part of the problem is that protein quality relative to equine feeding is a new subject, and there is still little information, next to no research, and a lot of historical misinformation. This knowledge gap will narrow in the next few years as research progresses.

Minerals

The mineral category is divided into two groups, macro and micro, to designate how much is needed in the diet.

Macro minerals are those generally involved in producing structural tissues. This group includes calcium, phosphorus, sodium, chloride, potassium, and magnesium. The nutritional requirements are usually expressed in percent or part per hundred.

Micro minerals are needed in much smaller amounts. Requirements are usually expressed in parts per million (ppm). These minerals are often involved as cofactors in enzyme systems such as hoof and hair growth, muscle contraction, and cartilage regeneration in joints. This group includes minerals such as copper, zinc, iodine, manganese, iron, selenium, cobalt, fluorine, chromium, and molybdenum.

For detailed information about supplementing minerals, refer to Chapter 4.

Calcium and Phosphorus

These two minerals comprise 70 percent of the horse's mineral requirements. They are essential in bones, but also play important roles in muscle function, nerve cell function, energy metabolism, cell membrane regulation, blood coagulation, and many other systems. Deficiencies of calcium (Ca) and phosphorus (P) are usually factors in problems with bones and joints. The body has a generous store of each of these in the skeleton.

As well as providing adequate amounts in the feed, calcium and phosphorus must also be present in the correct ratios. Too much phosphorus interferes with calcium uptake. A high level of calcium, on the other hand, does not cause a problem with phosphorus uptake, so it is considered better to have more calcium present than phosphorus. (Optimal requirements are provided in Table 4 of the Appendix.)

Calcium (Ca)

Because it is essential in the formation and hardening of bone, calcium is the mineral required in the greatest amounts. It is also a co-factor for many enzyme systems, for blood coagulation, glandular secretion, regulation of temperature, and the contraction of working muscle. Stored mostly in the skeleton, it can be found in every cell in the body.

Calcium is usually the first mineral that is "balanced for." Present in most feeds, it is readily available and can easily be supplemented.

Calcium must be present in the right ratio with phosphorus and with magnesium, as these minerals can interfere with absorption. It is now considered that optimal requirements for horses are 15–20 percent higher than those given in the National Research Council (NRC) tables.

Calcium is so important that its blood levels are tightly controlled by a number of hormones. The processes of absorption of calcium from the GI tract, excretion by the kidneys, and uptake and re-deposition of calcium and phosphorus in the bones are controlled by the hormones calcitonin, parathyroid, and cholecalciferol (Vitamin D).

Because 80 percent of the calcium in the body is stored in the skeleton, calcium deficiency appears primarily as bone and joint problems. Long-term mild deficiencies appear as swelling and softening of the non-weight-bearing bones, such as those of the face (Millers Disease, or Osteomalacia). Long-term major deficiencies will produce intermittent lameness and problems with weight-bearing bones.

Excess calcium leads to hardening of certain tissues, such as artery walls and other blood vessels. Excess calcium can interfere with zinc, manganese, and iron absorption and may cause symptoms of a deficiency of those minerals if their amounts in the diet are sufficient but marginal.

Assuming there is sufficient phosphorus in the diet, adult horses have been fed up to five times the recommended amounts of calcium without deleterious effects. Calcium supplementation is usually achieved by adding ground limestone ($CaCO_3$) to the ration or by adding legume hays. Legumes are much higher in calcium than grasses are.

Phosphorus (P)

Phosphorus is an essential component of nearly all enzyme systems and found in every cell in the body. Phosphorus is integral to the bones of the skeleton, which acts as the main body store. It must be in correct balance with calcium, referred to as the calcium:phosphorus ratio. Low phosphorus is usually found only when there are high levels of other minerals that interfere with uptake: for example, very high ratios of calcium (6:1) or high levels of aluminum.

Low phosphorus levels in the diet often create no immediate symptoms, as the body has a huge store in the skeleton and can withdraw phosphorus from the bones. A long-term deficiency in phosphorus results in bone and skeletal problems. Other common symptoms include weight loss, poor hair coat, and shifting lameness and bone problems.

There are no symptoms specific to high levels of phosphorus, as the body can easily rid itself of excesses of the mineral. High levels of phosphorus, however, interfere with calcium uptake. The symptoms of excessive phosphorus are therefore the same as for low calcium.

Magnesium (Mg)

Commonly written as Mg, magnesium is in the same family of minerals as calcium. It is an important ion, required by the body in relatively large amounts. It is essential for the optimal function of over 300 key enzymes involved in energy transformation, protein synthesis, and nucleic acid metabolism. It is also essential for the stability and normal function of the cell membranes of excitable tissues, such as nerve and muscle. Thus magnesium deficiencies or abnormalities have a profound effect on neuromuscular function and cardiac tissue. In addition, normal magnesium content is necessary for the maintenance of electrolyte balance, particularly for calcium and potassium.

As well as being important for the function of nerve and muscle, magnesium is involved in the formation of hydroxyapatite, one of the principal components of bone and a major "hardener" of bone. About 50 percent of the body's store of magnesium is found in the skeleton.

Since magnesium is intricately involved in muscle and nerve function, symptoms of magnesium deficiency usually include nervousness, an inability to concentrate, or an inability to relax muscles, as well as problems with carbohydrate metabolism, such as a tendency to founder.

Magnesium tends to be a very underrated mineral. Most nutrition books, unfortunately, say little about it.

Magnesium Physiology and Biochemistry

Clinical laboratories typically measure magnesium as total serum magnesium, of which around 50 percent is either bound to plasma protein or is complexed with ions such as phosphate or citrate. And around 50 percent is present in the ionized or active form. Although serum magnesium usually does not accurately reflect the overall body magnesium balance, deficiency symptoms correlate well with serum levels of <2.0 mg/dl or <1.5 mEq/l. In cattle, serum levels of below 2.0 mg/dl are associated with onset of grass tetany. Horses appear to be more resistant to low magnesium and very rarely develop outright grass tetany symptoms like ridgidity and inability to relax muscles. However, low serum magnesium levels are associated with symptoms of impaired muscle or nerve function. Refer to Chapter 8 for more information.

Magnesium, Pre-Cushings, and Founder

Some horses and ponies show symptoms of Pre-Cushings (PC) or Cushings-like Syndrome. The condition is characterized by lumpy, abnormal fat deposits on the neck, above the tail head, and on the shoulders. Unlike a true Cushings sufferer, these horses will usually have a normal level of Adreno-Cortical Stimulating Hormone (ACTH), but may well show elevated insulin. The horse may or may not have the typical extra thick hair coat, but the hair will

MAGNESIUM: THE NEGLECTED MINERAL

Magnesium is very important as a co-factor in enzymes that control the metabolism of carbohydrates, most specifically the enzymes that are involved in insulin response. Cells that are deficient in magnesium show impaired carbohydrate metabolism and a reduced insulin response.

Modern diets are often low in magnesium, at the same time that the high stress lifestyle of some equines leads to an increased need for magnesium. Areas with acid soils and soft water may not provide enough magnesium through natural sources for the needs of performance horses. The normal blood level for magnesium in horses is 2.2-2.7mg/dl; blood titers below 2.0 should be considered an indicator of low magnesium status. In a study at Virginia Polytechnic and State University in 1984, blood was drawn from all breeds and types of foals throughout Virginia, from the Blue Ridge Mountains to the Chesapeake Bay. The blood was assayed for mineral status; across the board, the magnesium levels were 1.8 -1.9 mg/dl, with some as low as 1.7mg/dl. This indicated a statewide incidence of low magnesium.

Such hypomagnesemia is prevalent up and down both coasts of the United States and anywhere there are clay soils or a granite base. Areas with a limestone base or alkaline soils have a less acute problem with low magnesium. The modern practice of using acid fertilizers as well as acid rain contribute to the problem of low soil magnesium, making it much harder for the plants to pull the magnesium out of the soil. Hence the apparent prevalence of hypomagnesemia we are seeing currently.

appear harsh and dull. There will be either a tendency to founder or a history of founder. These Pre-Cushings horses respond well to additional magnesium in their diets.

It should be noted that blood magnesium levels normally rise following glucose ingestion or following a meal high in simple carbohydrates, indicating that magnesium is involved with the action of insulin to clear the glucose from the blood. The Pre-Cushings horses can be considered the equivalent of a human type II diabetic. Type II diabetes is a resistance to insulin, rather than a true insulin deficiency. The Pre-Cushings horse may also show elevated insulin levels following a carbohydrate meal. These horses will do best if also fed a low glycemic diet (one low in simple carbohydrates); but the supplementation of magnesium will be beneficial even without the low glycemic diet. Refer to the section on Cushings in Chapter 8 for more on this diet.

Grass in the early spring is often low in minerals and high in sugar content. This may be why spring grass is often associated with founder in grazing horses and ponies. Magnesium may help to protect these horses from founder by protecting peripheral circulation to the foot and other extremities.

This response to magnesium in Pre-Cushings has not been established by scientific studies, and so far all evidence is anecdotal, but there is some precedent for this approach. Historically, an old horseman's trick is to give magnesium salts (usually magnesium sulphate, also known as Epsom salts) to horses that are foundering or in danger of foundering. The author has fed a magnesium supplement to over 1,000 Pre-Cushings horses so far and most have shown positive results, such as a reduction of the abnormal fatty deposits on the neck and shoulders, improvement in lameness scores, and a reduction in the incidence of founder attacks. While no statistical analysis of the work has been done, the evidence seems encouraging in such numbers of horses.

Magnesium and Tying-up Syndrome

Within the muscle cell, magnesium and calcium have antagonistic functions. Calcium ion is released during muscle contraction and binds to the actin-myosin complex, "locking" the muscle in the shortened or contracted state. When relaxation of the muscle is required, magnesium ions are released and "knock" the calcium from the binding site, allowing the actin–myosin complex to relax back to the inactive or noncontracted state. Hence low muscle levels of magnesium are associated with tetanic muscle states; for example, muscle spasms or muscles that cannot relax or return to the normal state. An excess of calcium or a deficiency of magnesium within the muscle cell, not necessarily in the diet, can both cause a temporary muscle tetany called tying-up or Recurrent Exertional Rhabdomyolosis (RER).

RER is associated with stress and anxiety in young horses in hard training and is characterized by a chronic tying-up (tetany) during work sessions. The incorrect level of the ions within the muscle cell is the cause of the tetany, not the levels in the diet, and this may be linked to a genetic enzyme deficiency, although the exact cause remains unclear at this time. Therefore, even if the diet appears to have adequate levels of magnesium, the condition will appear in horses predisposed to it. However, increasing the levels of magnesium has in some cases reduced the severity of the symptoms. Magnesium, which has an anti-anxiety effect, may help to

RER OR EPSM?

RER. This condition typically affects Thoroughbreds, Standardbreds, Arabs and other "hot blood" breeds. These horses are usually fit or partially fit, without access to turn-out. RER is seen most often in fillies of nervous temperament. The attacks occur about 15 to 20 minutes into the warm-up or exertion period. After the attack, the horse recovers slowly. These horses respond best to reductions of stress and anxiety, not necessarily to low glycemic diet, although that diet will help to some degree. Whether magnesium's anti-anxiety effect is physiological or psychological is not clear at this time. It could be due to the increased relaxation of muscle or some other mechanism which is not yet known.

EPSM. Typically, the EPSM horse has at least some draft horse or pony blood and is fat, unfit, and chunky, often with a placid temperament. Attacks occur in the beginning of the work session, and the horse is very slow to come out of it. Attacks are worse after a period of time in a stall. The horse responds well to the low glycemic diet.

alleviate stress and prevent RER from occurring. But the condition is more complicated than a simple deficiency of magnesium.

It is important to distinguish RER from the tying-up that is caused by an inability to handle simple carbohydrates, called Equine Polysaccharide Storage Myopathy (EPSM or EPSSM), as the latter condition is unlikely to respond to magnesium. EPSM should be handled with a low glycemic diet. (See Chapter 8.)

Clinically, magnesium has been used to treat cases of spontaneous smooth muscle contraction in humans. This includes conditions such as asthma, preeclampsia and eclampsia, seizures, and other problems with muscle spasms and arrhythmias.

Magnesium is easily absorbed from the GI tract and may have at least one carrier that is magnesium specific and one that is competitive with calcium. Hence magnesium and calcium in the diet need to be balanced, the ideal ratio being 1:1. In practical fact, calcium is usually well supplied in horse diets and magnesium tends to be low, so it is considered better to supplement the magnesium and assume that the diet will provide sufficient calcium.

Magnesium Supplementation

Magnesium can be supplied in various forms. There are several magnesium salts readily available, but the preferred supplements offer the chelated forms. Chelation means the magnesium is bound to a highly absorbable molecule like an amino acid. As the amino acid is picked up from the GI tract, the magnesium comes with it. Although non-organic forms of magnesium salts are well absorbed, the presence of other minerals like calcium may interfere with absorption. The non-chelated forms are usually cheaper and can supply useful magnesium at low cost, but for therapeutic use to address a health concern, the chelated forms are more effective.

The most common form available is magnesium sulfate ($MgSO_4$), commonly called Epsom salts. Epsom salts can be a useful source of magnesium on an emergency basis, but are not suitable for regular feeding. One side effect of regular feeding of Epsom salts is high GI tract motility, or diarrhea. The preferred form used in animal feeds is magnesium oxide (MgO), a fine white powder. Magnesium oxide is about 50 percent absorbable, depending on the relative levels of calcium also present.

Normally, magnesium is non-toxic and is impossible to over-dose by mouth. The GI tract absorbs what it needs and the rest is excreted. Excess MgO or $MgSO_4$ produces a transient diarrhea while the GI tract dumps the excess. Therefore, over-feeding magnesium in the form of salts just results in expensive manure.

Kidney Impairment Caution

The main pathway for the deposition of magnesium is via the kidneys. Salts of magnesium are very water-soluble and magnesium is readily excreted, but if renal function is impaired, there may result an inability to dispose of magnesium and hence an overdose. Therefore, magnesium salts should not be fed to horses with impaired kidney function or those with restricted water intakes. Symptoms of excess magnesium intake are depression, muscle flaccidity, and uncoordinated gaits.

All About Electrolytes

Sodium chloride, along with salts of potassium, magnesium, and other ions, are often referred to as electrolytes. In terms of horse nutrition, an electrolyte is a substance that the horse needs for normal function but which is lost through sweat when horses are working, especially in hot, humid weather, and which needs to be supplied in the feed or free choice to compensate for those losses.

Sodium

Both sodium (Na) and chloride (Cl) are minerals that are required by the horse for the regulation of body fluids, for acid–base balance, for transmission of nerve cell signals, and for maintenance of cell membrane potential. For maintenance, the horse needs 0.1 percent sodium in the diet, increased to 0.3 percent if it is pregnant or in work. The maintenance requirement can be supplied by adding common table salt (39 percent Na, 61 percent Cl) at a rate of one-quarter of 1 percent of the weight of the feed. However, because this mineral is one for which horses have a ready appetite, as long as the mineral is offered free choice, the horse will generally consume what it needs.

Potassium

Potassium (K) is essential for cellular functioning. Along with sodium, it is involved with the transmission of nerve signals and in regulation of cellular membranes. Potassium is usually well supplied in all forages. Only hard working horses that sweat heavily need extra potassium. Horses that have the genetic condition Hyper-kalemic Periodic Paralysis (HYPP) are unable to handle potassium and need to be fed diets as low as possible in potassium, which is challenging, as nearly all feeds have an ample supply. See Chapter 8 for more information.

ELECTROLYTES DEFINED

Chemically, an electrolyte is defined as a micro-molecule that will dissociate to form positive (+) and negative (-) ions when placed in solution and is thus capable of conducting electricity.

Electrolytes are involved in nerve transmission, muscle contraction, and regulation of water flow in the body. If there is too great a loss of electrolyte ions in the sweat, muscle and nerve function are compromised. The horse may become unable to continue and can get very sick and possibly die. The main ion that is of concern is potassium (K+), but calcium, sodium, magnesium, chloride, and bicarbonate are also involved.

Low potassium in blood and tissue due to sweat losses can produce the very frightening and potentially dangerous conditions called "thumps." In this condition, a syncronicity of heart contraction and diaphragm muscle contraction produces a loud thumping noise, as well as interfering with normal breathing. The condition is dramatic and frightening and if left untreated can be dangerous. To confuse the issue, some of the latest research seems to indicate that calcium ions have a role to play in this condition as well, but exactly how and where is not yet clear.

Very severe losses of potassium can compromise the function of cardiac muscle, putting the horse at considerable risk.

Loss of magnesium means that the muscles have problems relaxing following exertion and may lock in tight convulsions, called tetany, which are painful.

Supplementation is usually from the salt potassium chloride, which is obtainable in the product Lite Salt. Potassium requirements are given in Table 4 of the Appendix.

Because there is no supply of stored electrolytes in the body, it is important that they be provided in the feed or in an additional bucket of drinking water containing added electrolytes both prior to strenuous work and again afterwards to make sure the horse consumes adequate levels to replenish losses. The best way to achieve this is via a commercial electrolyte mix. The mix should contain the minerals in the same proportions that are lost in sweat. (See table below.) Note the very high levels of potassium and magnesium in the sweat relative to the plasma. This means that an electrolyte mix should contain almost as much potassium and magnesium as it does sodium.

COMPOSITION OF SWEAT AND PLASMA (MMOL/L)

	SWEAT	PLASMA
Na+	131.8	140.0
Cl-	174.4	100.0
K+	53.1	3.8
Ca++(i)	6.2	6.0
Mg++	4.6	1.8

Most commercial electrolyte mixes are fine, if a little low in magnesium and high in sugar. If you want to make your own, here are some formulae. Or you can add 20 grams of magnesium oxide to balance a commercial mix.

Formulae for Electrolyte Solutions

Formula #1
40g common table salt (NaCl)
30g "Lite" salt (KCl)
20g Magnesium oxide or magnesium sulphate (Epsom salts)
Approximately 2 gallons of water

To allow the horse to replace the salts as it drinks, offer a bucket of the electrolyte solution in addition to normal water. It helps if you also add some kind of sweet fruit drink or crystal-drink flavoring to make it taste better. Horses like the taste of the sugar and thus will drink it more readily. Apple juice is a favorite, or whatever flavoring the horse likes and is used to.

It is important that this bucket of electrolyte solution be offered in addition to the normal drinking water. Some horses may not drink it and thus would become dehydrated without an alternative. Once the horse is accustomed to the taste, he will usually drink it freely. If you can't or don't want to make the liquid electrolyte solution, then add 3 ounces of the dry mix per day to the feed. Offer electrolytes daily during very hot weather, whenever the horse is sweating profusely, or for two days prior to and following strenuous exercise.

Horses **do not** choose their feed on the basis of what they need nutritionally any more than we do; they choose based on the taste and, like us, they prefer sweet and salty flavors. So if you offer this blend free choice, the probability is that the horse will not consume enough unless you add sugar or sweetener. Magnesium sulfate in particular does not taste very nice, so if the horse consistently rejects the mix, try adding magnesium oxide instead.

Formula #2
1 pt Dolomitic limestone (Mg/Ca Carbonate)
2 pts table salt (iodized is best) (NaCl)
1 pt "Lite" salt (KCl)
Mix together and then add 2 ounces of mix per gallon of water. If the horse does not like the taste, add some Kool-Aid powder at about one-third normal strength to make it more palatable. To be sure the horse will drink the Kool-Aid flavor you choose *before* you get to the competition, offer him some at home until he is used to it.

Micro-minerals: Less Is Best

While the macro-minerals are generally measured in percentage (parts per hundred) or grams, the micro-minerals are measured in parts per million (ppm) or in milligrams per kilogram of feed (mg/kg) — the two measurements are in fact the same. Confusingly, some texts give the requirement as mg per kg body weight. But it is more usual to give it as mg/kg feed. In this text we will refer to it as mg/kg feed or ppm.

The easiest but least effective way to supply trace minerals is to offer a good quality trace mineralized salt, in either a block form or added to feed. A better but more expensive method is to feed chelated minerals. These are usually available in specialized mineral supplements. It is unusual to find the chelated forms in general feeds due to the expense.

Chromium (Cr)

Chromium is involved in enzymes of carbohydrate metabolism and may play a role in the response of cells to insulin. It has been used with some success in horses that show glucose intolerance and insulin resistance. An inability to respond to insulin in horses (similar to Type II diabetes in humans) has symptoms that look a lot like Cushings disease, also producing a tendency to founder.

The dietary requirement for chromium has yet to be established in the horse. However, the dose that alleviates the symptoms in these Cushings-like horses is 200 ppb or .2mg /kg feed per day.

Cobalt (Co)

Cobalt is involved together with the enzyme cyanocobalmin (Vitamin B12) in the intestinal absorption of iron. In humans, low cobalt produces a form of anemia called pernicious anemia, but this has not been evident in the horse. There are no known toxicity symptoms for cobalt in the horse. The requirement is generally considered to be 0.1 ppm per weight of dietary dry matter.

This amount was derived from ruminant research, and the optimal requirement in horses is not known.

Copper (Cu)

Copper is involved in the formation and maturation of several different kinds of connective tissue, including collagen and elastin, as well as cartilage. It helps in the mobilization of iron reserves and in the formation of the pigment melanin. Anemia and loss of pigment due to low copper is well known in ruminants, but is less well documented in horses. There have been a few cases of depigmentation in black or liver chestnut horses that were resolved by increasing copper levels in the diet.

Low copper has been shown to increase the number of *osteochondrosis dissecans* (OCD) lesions in young horses. OCD lesions are malformations of the cartilage and underlying bone in the joints. In two studies, foals fed 7 and 15 ppm of copper had many more OCD lesions as compared to foals fed 30 and 50 ppm.

Horses are much less susceptible to high copper levels than ruminants are; in one study, ponies were able to graze and thrive on land that had copper levels high enough to kill lambs. The upper safe limit is usually considered to be 2,800 ppm (mg/kg).

Copper is usually added to the ration as copper sulfate, but there are now the chelated forms available that are much more absorbable. Copper requirements are not well defined by the National Research Council. Most feeds contain 3-20 ppm (mg/kg); the NRC recommends 10 ppm for all ages of horses, which may well be too low for growing youngsters. It is recommended to include 50 ppm in foal feeds and weanling rations.

Fluorine (F)

The presence of fluorine affects bones and teeth. A deficiency of fluoride has yet to be observed in the horse, but a toxicosis called fluorosis has been seen in young horses. The symptoms nearly always involve the bones and teeth, with the most common symptom being mottling or discoloration and damage to the teeth. The teeth can deteriorate to the point where the animal will not eat or drink enough, so symptoms look like general debilitation.

In adult horses whose teeth are already formed, exposure to high fluorine will not affect the teeth. In older horses, the symptoms appear to be a poor or unthrifty appearance, with a rough, dry, dull hair coat. As the fluorosis develops, the horse will become stiff and lame and may show thickening and malformation of the bones and the feet.

Fluorosis occurs where phosphate fertilizers are used that have been insufficiently defluorinated, or down wind of smelting plants or metal processing plants where the fluorine released from the plant contaminates the soil, the plants, and the water in the area. Otherwise it is not common.

Iodine (I)

Iodine is involved with thyroxine, a hormone which controls basal metabolism. There are two forms of thyroxine, tri-iodothyroxine (T3) and tera-iodothyroxine (T4). These two forms of the hormone are produced and stored in the thyroid gland. A deficiency of iodine interferes with production, and the preliminary form of thyroxine accumulates; the gland swells and produces the condition called goiter. Confusingly, an excess of iodine also interferes in thyroxine production by negative feedback, causing accumulation of thyroxine. The gland swells in response. Thus, both a deficiency and an excess of iodine produce the same symptoms. These symptoms can include dry, rough hair coat, increased susceptibility to infections due to a poorly functioning immune system, lethargy, dullness, drowsiness, timidity, an inability to withstand cold, and, in advanced cases, a thickening of the skin called myxodema. Because there is no effective laboratory test, the only way to tell whether one is dealing with a deficiency or excess is to analyze the diet and calculate the iodine intake.

Most overdoses occur because of the addition of extra iodine to rations in an attempt to overcome various problems that might respond to iodine. (This is a common practice in other farm livestock, but horses are more susceptible to iodine overdose). Overdose can also occur in horses fed seaweed or seaweed-based supplements in addition to feeds that already contain iodine.

There are plants that contain substances that bind up the iodine and make it unavailable; if these plants are eaten, they can also cause a deficiency. The effect of these plants can be overcome by increasing iodine intake. Examples of plants that bind iodine are kale, turnips, rutabaga, and other plants of the Brassicaceae family.

The easiest way to increase iodine intake is to feed iodized salt. As little as half an ounce (14g) per day of iodized salt will supply adequate iodine for a horse. However, in horses fed salt free-choice, there is considerable variation in salt intake. This is why there can be both iodine-deficient foals and normal foals in the same herd, when they are fed the same diet but offered iodized salt free-choice. Therefore, it is recommended to feed non-iodized salt free-choice and add iodized salt to the feed.

The thyroid gland, the placenta, and the mammary glands all tend to accumulate iodine. Goiters appear occasionally in newborn foals whose dams were over-supplied with iodine, which can happen even if the mare does not show any symptoms of excess. In general, this condition is self-limiting; the goiter goes down as the foal starts to take its nutrition from the mare's milk, which is much less likely to have high iodine content. In this situation, it is important to reduce the iodine supplementation to the mare until the goiter disappears.

Iodine requirements are considered to be 1-2mg/horse/day; 5 mg/horse/day is excessive and harmful.

Iron (Fe)

Iron is essential to hemoglobin, the main oxygen carrier in blood. Low iron results in a condition called anemia. True anemia due to low iron in feed is very rare in horses. Anemia is commonly related to chronic blood loss from either lice and tick infestations or worms. Excessive iron levels in the feed or water can result in increased susceptibility to bacterial infection and to joint problems.

Requirements in horses are generally considered to be 50 ppm for pregnancy, growth, and lactation and 40 ppm for all others. Most forages contain 50–400 ppm iron, and cereal grains contain 30–90 ppm, so iron is usually present in ample amounts in the diet.

Molybdenum (Mo)

Molybdenum is very similar in function to copper, as it is also involved in several pathways, including the generation of cartilage and connective tissue. A true deficiency of molybdenum in the horse has yet to be identified. The requirement is believed to be less than 0.1 ppm (mg/kg). The primary concern is overdosing. High intakes of molybdenum can cause interference with copper uptake and utilization. High intakes typically occur in animals grazing where the land has been contaminated with industrial waste or metals. This occurrence is so rare that there is no specific test. Diagnosis is typically arrived at by inference rather than direct measurement after symptoms attributed to low copper levels don't respond to increased copper in the diet.

Selenium (Se)

This mineral plays a role in several essential enzyme systems, most notably those involved in muscle function and in the thyroid gland. It is also a component of the enzyme glutathione peroxidase. Glutathione peroxidase along with vitamin E provides important antioxidant protection for cell membranes. Selenium (Se) is very closely associated with vitamin E, and both must be supplied in adequate amounts. However, you can feed slightly less vitamin E if there is sufficient selenium, and vice versa.

Horses require around 0.1 ppm (mg/kg) in their diet. This amount is usually doubled to 0.2 ppm for working horses, pregnant mares in their last trimester, and growing foals. Intakes of over 150 ppm are toxic. Nearly all minerals have the potential to be overdosed, but avoiding this is most critical in the case of selenium. The maximum recommended intake is 2 ppm.

Most states in the United States have a selenium deficiency in their soils. This is particularly true where soils are acidic, since in alkaline soils selenium is better absorbed by plants. However, some plants in the western United States accumulate selenium, such as milkvetches, goldenweeds, Prince's Plume, asters, saltbrush, and Indian paintbrush. If they are ingested, they produce acute selenium toxicity, or alkali disease. But in general, if selenium toxicity occurs, it is because of miscalculation and oversupplementation in the diet (or by injection) rather than by ingestion of plants.

Deficiency symptoms vary considerably depending on the degree of the deficiency. Signs can range from mild, such as poor or compromised immune system seen as increased susceptibility to infection, poor growth in foals, and lowered fertility in mares and stallions, to the extreme, such as muscle wasting, damage, and death seen in severely deficient foals. The muscle damage and inflamed fatty deposits evident in severe selenium deficiency is called white muscle disease. Adding selenium to the diet in the early stages of the disease can be corrective, but early diagnosis is rare. In adult horses with low selenium, the symptoms can include stiffness and sore muscles, with an inability to recover from exertion.

Selenium Supplementation

Supplementation of selenium can be delivered via selenised salt (a salt block containing 90 ppm Se), but is probably best accomplished by adding both vitamin E and a selenium source to the feed. The usual method is to add sodium selenite, but there is now a form of chelated selenium. The chelated form has selenium bound to the amino acid methionine; the resulting seleno-methionine, although it is more expensive, is both more absorbable and less toxic than the sodium selenite.

Sulfur (S)

Sulfur is part of the group of amino acids including cystine, cysteine, and methionine; these amino acids are integral in forming hair, hooves, and skin, as well as many other proteins. Sulfur can be supplied in the form of methylsulfonymethane (MSM) and best supplied in the organic forms of either the amino acids or in MSM (see section on protein). (Non-ruminants like horses cannot utilize inorganic sulfur, such as that found in sulfated salt blocks.) Requirement is considered to be 0.15% or more of organic sulfur.

Excess organic sulfur has no reported symptoms. However, in one situation where horses were accidentally fed over 300g of inorganic sulfur, they showed symptoms of lethargy and colic, followed by yellow frothy discharge from the nose, jaundice (yellowing of whites of the eye and other mucous membranes), and labored breathing. In two cases, the sulfur toxicity proved fatal.

Zinc (Zn)

Zinc is active in several enzyme systems, predominantly those involved in carbohydrate metabolism and also those involved with protein synthesis and gene expression. The NRC recommends 40mg/kgBW (body weight) intake for all classes of horses. However, studies have shown that foals fed higher levels (up to 152mg/kg) of zinc had lower incidence of Developmental Orthopedic Disease (DOD) than those fed lower levels. So the 40mg level may be considered inadequate for young growing horses. In foals and weanlings 60mg/kg may be a better level.

Excess zinc levels interfere with copper uptake; the symptoms of zinc excess are the same as a deficiency of copper (see pages 48–49). Most cases of zinc toxicity occur down-wind of smelters, mines, or brass foundries or where pastures have been top-dressed with zinc oxide. Correcting for excess zinc is impossible, and death is the usual result.

Vitamins

Vitamins are organic substances that the body requires for various biological processes, but which the body may not synthesize adequately to meet its requirements. So vitamins must be supplied in the diet either as the substance itself or as a precursor molecule.

Horses grazing on a good grass pasture and receiving two to three hours of sunlight daily will require very little by way of vitamin supplementation.

They are divided into two groups: the water-soluble vitamins — vitamin C and vitamins B1 through 12 — and the fat-soluble vitamins — A, D, E, and K. Of the fat-soluble vitamins, only A and E cannot be synthesized by the horse's body and must therefore be supplied.

Nearly all the vitamins are well supplied by green grass and sunlight. Horses grazing on a good grass pasture and getting two to three hours of sunlight daily will require very little by way of vitamin supplementation. Vitamins stored in the body last a few months, so even a couple of weeks of cloudy weather won't create a deficiency. However, horses that live with limited turnout or in stalls and who eat mostly preserved grass in the form of hay or silage will require supplementation. A few categories of horses with exceptionally high requirements, such as growing foals, pregnant or lactating mares, and horses in hard training, will often show improved appearance and condition if they are supplemented with certain vitamins, even though their diet may appear to be adequate.

There is a difference in effectiveness between the minimum level (the lowest level below which deficiency symptoms appear) and the optimum level (the level at which the horse shows an improved appearance or condition). The optimum level is often considerably higher than the minimum level. The NRC tables generally provide the minimum levels, so there is some argument for increasing the levels of certain vitamins in the equine diet. The amounts provided in this book are closer to the optimum levels.

All vitamins have toxic levels: that is, levels above which certain deleterious conditions may begin to appear. This is more likely for the fat-soluble vitamins, which are much harder to excrete and thus can accumulate in the body if overfed for a considerable period. The water-soluble vitamins are much easier for the body to get rid of and are correspondingly less likely to accumulate.

The Water-Soluble Vitamins: B_{1-12} & C

Water-soluble vitamins are produced in the hind-gut and are likely to be adequately available in those horses receiving adequate fiber in their diet. However, hard-working horses or very young foals may experience shortages due to insufficient hind-gut activity.

NUTRITION FOR SOUND HOOF GROWTH

"No foot, no horse" is a well-known phrase that still holds true today. Many otherwise sound horses have been rendered unusable because their feet cannot retain shoes, bruise easily, or are generally weak. While horn quality is strongly affected by genetics (parents with strong feet generally produce offspring with strong feet), it is possible, within limits, to improve the quality of horn growth with appropriate nutrition and hoof care.

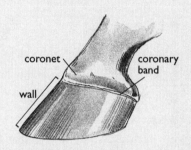

It helps to understand how the hoof grows. The horn of the walls of the foot consists of the same keratin protein from which hair is made. Keratin is produced by a special layer of cells in the coronary band above the hoof called the coronary corium and by the inner layer of laminae cells within the foot. As

Healthy feet need the right mix of nutrients.

the horn cells in the coronary band and laminae produce the keratin, the horn expands outwards from the laminae and down from the coronary band towards the ground, forming a double thickness of hoof wall. *It takes four to six months for the horn at the top of the foot to grow down to the base, where it holds the nails. It takes three to four weeks for the inner wall to grow outwards to thicken the layer just inside the wall.*

The best bet to improve the quality of the horn is a two-pronged approach.

1. *Regular* shoeing by a good farrier: every four to six weeks for most horses.

2. Proper nutrition, which will supply the reproducing horn cells with the raw materials they need for growth.

If the cells do not receive what they need when they need it, the horn will be of poorer quality than if all the ingredients were present.

If your horse has weak, shelly, or crumbly feet that don't hold nails well, you need to feed supplements that contain the following ingredients: biotin, methionine, zinc, fatty acids, and sometimes sulfur. The important ingredient in methionine is sulfur, which is part of the molecular "glue" and can be supplied in its organic form by the supplement MSM.

The Key Ingredients For Horn Growth

• Good quality protein will supply the amino acid methionine. It provides sulfur, the "glue" that holds the keratin strands together.

• Biotin is a B vitamin that is an integral part of the enzyme chain that produces the keratin in the cells. If biotin is insufficient, hoof growth proceeds very slowly, even if enough methionine is present.

• Zinc, a co-enzyme, is an essential component of the enzyme system that produces protein.

• A good supply of fatty acids provides much of the raw material for the horn.

You may have to buy more than one supplement to obtain all of the above nutrients. To know what a supplement contains, carefully read the ingredient label or ask the manufacturer.

For the Best Hoof Growth

1. Buy horses of a breed noted for sound feet, or descended from bloodlines bred for hoof health.

2. Find an accomplished farrier and schedule regular visits: not once in a while, but every four to six weeks.

3. Feed good quality supplement(s) that contain *all* of the key ingredients listed above in combination, not just one or two of them.

It takes four to six months for the new horn to grow down to the point where the shoe nails pass through it. You must feed a supplement for at least 16 weeks to achieve any benefit, although you will see a change in the horn of the upper part of the foot in six to eight weeks. Since the horn grows down from the top of the hoof, horn that is already in place cannot be much affected by nutrition.

The only effect you can have on existing horn quality is to keep it sufficiently moist to retain its integrity and strength. The periople, a layer of natural varnish, grows from the perioplic corium to cover the surface of the horn and minimizes moisture loss from the hoof. This periople is rasped away by the farrier when he trims the foot for shoeing. Some materials can act as a varnish to impede loss of moisture from the top (replacing the periople), but all the hoof dressings in the world can only help retain existing strength. You cannot increase the tensile strength beyond that which the horn started out with. Be aware that too much dressing will weaken the "glue" between the keratin strands and hence weaken the hoof wall.

Horses in very hard work will benefit from additional B vitamins, especially folic acid, in their diet. Very debilitated horses or horses not getting enough fiber in their diet (which adversely affects hind-gut fermentation) may also have deficiencies. Horses on certain oral antibiotics or other medications may also benefit from supplementation, as these medications may interfere with the microbial activity and thus impair production of the B vitamins.

The B vitamins are thiamine (B1), riboflavin (B2), niacin, pyridoxine (B6), pantothenic acid (B3), folic acid, biotin, choline, and cyanocobalamin (B12). Thiamine and riboflavin are involved with nerve function, and a deficiency can show as nervousness and hyperexcitability. Some people claim that supplementing a nervous or excitable horse with extra thiamine helps it to calm down and relax. This approach works even better if thiamine is combined with magnesium supplementation.

Folic acid may be beneficial, especially for stabled horses or those in hard work. While no specific symptoms of folic acid deficiency have been identified in the horse, a folic acid deficiency in pigs results in decreased red blood cell counts. To address poor performance in horses in hard training, it might be worthwhile to supplement with folic acid.

The B vitamin biotin is associated with keratin production. Keratin is an important constituent of hoof and hair. Horses who show poor or weak hoof growth can benefit from supplementation that includes biotin. Although it is common for hoof growth supplements to contain biotin, this vitamin is not all that is required.

Vitamin C

Vitamin C, or ascorbic acid, is synthesized in the horse's liver from glucose, so it is not usually necessary to supplement equine diets with vitamin C. It is also available in green foods. However, horses that have no access to fresh green grass or that are subject to a lot of stress, such as traveling to shows or shipping long distances, may benefit from additional vitamin C. If the horse is under stress, supplementing with vitamin C will provide an immune system boost. But because the horse can adequately synthesize it, a true deficiency has yet to be reported.

The Fat-Soluble Vitamins: A, D, E, K

Vitamin A, also known as beta-carotene, is derived from carotene, a plant pigment. (This is yet another reason why green and orange colored feeds should be provided.) Vitamin A has an interreaction with vitamin E, which increases the absorption and utilization of vitamin A and can minimize vitamin A toxicity in case of an over-dose from excessive supplementation. It is usually worth supplementing vitamin A to horses that are stabled and receive only hay, especially breeding horses and horses in hard training. Low levels of vitamin A are associated with infertility, but there is no hard evidence that extra vitamin A increases fertility in normally fed horses.

Recommended amounts of vitamin A in horses are 2,000–3,000 IU (international units) per day. Carotenes in growing pasture can provide up to 120,000–240,000 IU. In good hay the content can reach 8,000– 16,000 IU; in poor-quality hay, the content is around 1,600–2,000 IU. Thus, as long as the horse gets access to green pasture or good quality hay, ample vitamin A will be available. If only poor-quality hay is available, then the horse may need supplementation. To learn the vitamin value of your hay, it is best to have it analyzed by your local extension office.

Vitamin D, or cholecalciferol, is involved in the control of calcium in the body. It can be synthesized in the skin from cholesterol precursors. There are considerable stores of it in the liver. It is rarely low in animals that are out in the sun and grazing green grass. Occasionally horses that are kept in all the time and who do not get good hay experience a deficiency. Turnout in sunshine and access to green grass are the best ways to resupply vitamin D. For horses that live indoors, ensure an ample supply of good hay and at least a few hours turnout in sunshine.

Vitamin E, or alpha-tocopherol, is derived from plant oils and some plant pigments, as well as whole grains and molasses. The recommended intake is 50–100 IU per day, though a conservative maximum has been set at 1,000 IU/kg diet. Vitamin E is very closely involved with selenium, and the two are usually supplemented together. Vitamin E is usually worth supplementing, especially to working horses or those who live in stalls.

There are no overdose symptoms for vitamin E reported for horses. In general, vitamin E is more likely to be undersupplied. Vitamin E is often used in better class feeds as an antioxidant, and the horse's requirements can be well met with such feeds. Synthetic forms of vitamin E (listed as dl-alpha-tocopherol), which are sometimes used as feed preservatives, are not bioavailable. Use natural forms of vitamin E, such as found in green plants, as the basis for filling vitamin E requirements.

MAIN NUTRIENTS AND THEIR USES

NUTRIENT	USED FOR
Carbohydrates	Energy supply for working muscles, red cells, and kidney medulla. Main energy storage for muscles. Precursor for basic molecules and for many enzyme systems.
Proteins	Basic building blocks for cell, enzymes, cell contents. Matrix of bone. Made of amino acids.
Fats	Formation of cell membranes, energy storage, and production and transmittal of essential enzymes; precursor of essential hormones.
Vitamin A	Precursor for eye pigments and various membranes.
Vitamin D	Involved in calcium control.
Vitamin E	Antioxidant, precursor for membranes.
Vitamin B complex	Precursor for enzymes of energy metabolism, protein synthesis, and other essential systems.
Vitamin C	Antioxidant and immunity booster.
Vitamin K	Essential cofactor for blood clotting.

MINERALS	
Macro:	
Calcium, Phosphorus	Bones, teeth, general cell function.
Magnesium	Bones, muscle function, nerve function.
Potassium, Sodium	General health of cells, electrolytes.
Micro:	
Iron, Iodine, Zinc, Copper, Selenium, Manganese, Cobalt	Enzyme systems, protein synthesis, cartilage, growth, carbohydrate metabolism, connective tissues, general health.

Vitamin K is present in the diet and is also produced in adequate amounts in the hind-gut, so it is rarely supplemented in horse diets. Vitamin K is involved in blood clotting. Horses on anticoagulant treatment may need to be monitored carefully; an overdose of anticoagulant or other blood thinners can be offset by additional vitamin K. In cases of excessive ingestion of anticoagulants either by accident or overdose, call your vet.

-3-

What to
Feed and Why

HORSES ARE PRIMARILY FIBER DIGESTERS and the bulk of their feed should consist of fiber, which provides valuable complex carbohydrates like cellulose. As discussed in Chapters 1 and 2, the importance of fiber in a horse's diet should not be underestimated. Many of the so-called management issues common with many horses, from behavioral concerns like spookiness and cribbing to health issues like founder and tying-up, can often be attributed to a lack of fresh grasses or other forage feeds in the horse's diet. In addition, excessive feeding of concentrates, often resorted to in an effort to compensate when horses are primarily kept in stalls and fed minimal natural fiber sources, can exacerbate such management issues.

Concentrates are defined as any feed or mix of feeds that are high in digestible energy and low in fiber, such as straight cereal grains, a blend of cereal grains, or a commercial formula, usually blended with a variety of additives. Some concentrates supply energy in the form of starch, some in the form of fat. Some feeds will supply protein and some will supply a mixture of these.

Don't necessarily assume that anything that goes into the feed bucket is a concentrate and anything fed from a hay rack is not, because in terms of nutrient content there is no clearly defined line between a concentrate and a forage. Some feeds that are high in fiber fall into a sort of gray area: neither one nor the other. As you will see in this chapter, feeding the horse is a matter of balancing the various contributions so that, overall, the horse receives a blend that matches what he needs. To mirror the best approach to feeding your horse, the discussion of forage comes first.

Forage Feeds

High-fiber feeds are known as roughage or forage; there are several types:
- Fresh, as in pasture grasses
- Preserved, as in hay or silage
- Preserved by drying and then ground and used in mixed feeds, such as alfalfa meal
- Preserved as hay cubes, usually alfalfa that has been dried and compressed
- Ground high-fiber by-products from grains processed for human consumption. (These high-fiber by-products are often added to concentrate rations to aid digestion and provide required fiber in the concentrate.)

Fresh Forage

While many different plants grow in a typical pasture, we usually divide plant types into two groups: grasses or legumes. Grasses can be further divided into cool-season or warm-season grasses. As the name implies, cool-season grasses grow best where summer temperatures are lower. These temperate region grasses can survive freezing and are common in the north. Warm-season grasses grow best where there is little or no winter frost and can survive higher summer temperatures. Cool-season grasses are generally more palatable, but in the hot summers of the south, when the only grazing or forage available consists of warm-season grasses, horses will graze them. Cool-season grasses include timothy, orchard grass, fescue, bluegrass, and redtop. Warm-season grasses include such species as brome, Coastal Bermuda, and Tift 44. Certain warm-season grasses, such as Sudan grass, Johnson grass, and Sorghum grass, can be toxic to horses and should be eliminated.

For grazing animals, grasses are a major source of both energy and protein; at some stages in their growth cycle, grasses can be

COOL-SEASON GRASSES

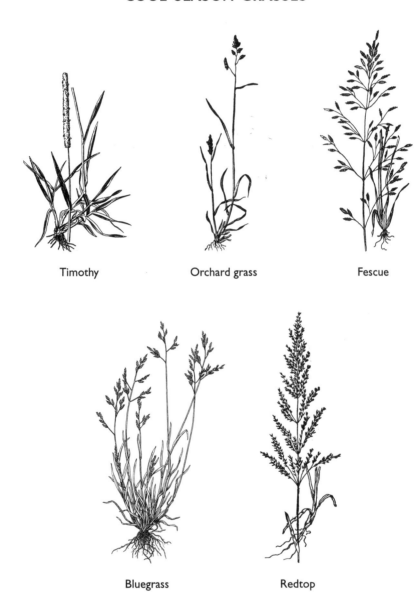

Timothy   Orchard grass   Fescue

Bluegrass   Redtop

There are literally thousands of species of grasses, and more are developed every year. For a current list of available types of grasses, contact your state extension office.

WARM-SEASON GRASSES

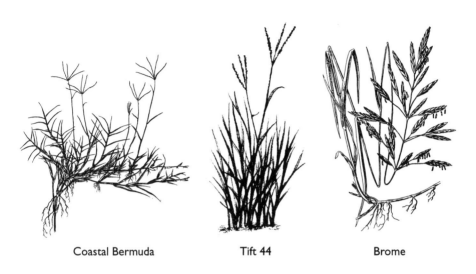

Coastal Bermuda   Tift 44   Brome

TOXIC GRASSES

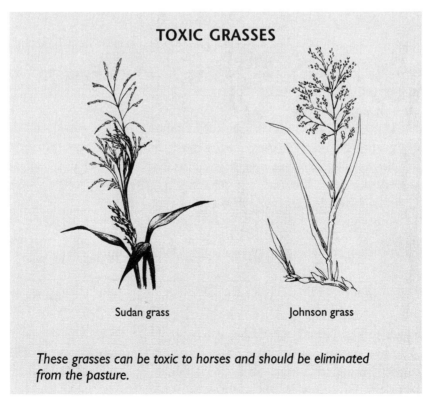

Sudan grass   Johnson grass

These grasses can be toxic to horses and should be eliminated from the pasture.

very high in energy and are often overlooked as a source of nutrition. They tend to supply less protein and more fiber, except in the early spring when they begin to grow. In that phase, the grass is high in sugar and low in fiber. Horses that are Pre-Cushinoid (see Chapter 8) or insulin resistant should be kept off the spring grass until it has at least flowered or, preferably, seeded, a topic further discussed in Chapter 8. Once the grass reaches the flowering stage, the fiber content increases and the mineral levels rise. Grasses that have gone to seed offer a low energy content and a very high fiber content. They can be almost indigestible because of the high lignin levels they produce once they have seeded. But mature grass can still offer a good source of fiber and some energy.

Legumes include such plants as alfalfa, lespedeza, and the various clovers, such as white, red, sweet, and alsike clover. Alsike clover is not a desirable plant as it can cause photosensitivity during hot, humid weather. Red clover can cause slobbering when grazed in the summer months. Both photosensitivity and slobbering are result from a mold that grows on the clovers in hot, humid weather. The best answer is to remove horses from the pasture for a few hours a day and give them hay that does not contain clovers. Slobbering is rarely a major health problem, but many people find it unsightly and unpleasant. To stop it altogether, disallow grazing entirely and feed hay.

Hays made from clovers are safe, however, if they are produced early enough in the year, before the weather becomes hot and humid. A first cut of clover hay is fine, but a first cut that is harvested late or a second cut presents a potential problem. See Chapter 8 for more information on feed toxins.

Legumes obtain nitrogen from the air via root nodules and thus require far less fertilizer than grasses do. They also produce a higher level of protein in their leaves. Therefore, hay made from them supplies a high protein level, a fact that needs to be considered when balancing legume hay with the rest of the ration. This may mean adding extra fiber into the ration by supplying a grass hay with lower protein values, or even clean straw as an added fiber source. Another option is to balance it with a concentrate ration that is higher in fiber and lower in protein. Legumes also tend to be high in calcium and low in phosphorus, so mixing them with grass hay can help to balance the calcium/phosphorus ratio. (See Chapter 4 to learn how to balance your overall feeding program.)

Factoring in Pasture

The contribution of the pasture to the overall feed ration should be taken into account, though usually it isn't. Pasture is usually considered as a substitute for hay in ration balancing. A horse will consume between 1.5 and 3 percent of its body weight per day in dry matter (DM). In one study, horses grazing for three hours on tall fescue consumed 3.3 pounds; when grazing alfalfa for the same period, they consumed 3.63 pounds.

The food value of pasture plants that a horse eats in any given period of time depends on the maturity of the plants, availability, and palatability. Because grass plants are most palatable when they are in the early stages of growth, the keys to getting the most out of grazing are:

1. Not to allow over-grazing;

2. Rotating the pastures, allowing time for the resting pastures to regenerate some growth; and

3. Mowing the pastures to reduce old growth and encourage new growth.

Chapter 7 provides detailed information on managing your pastures.

When estimating the feed value of pasture grazing as you calculate feed rations, allow between three-quarters and one pound of dry matter per hour of grazing, if the pastures are in good shape and there is plenty of young growth. In older pastures, allow between one-quarter and one half-pound per hour of grazing. Identify the most common species of grass in your pasture and use the National Research Council (NRC) tables to obtain the average feed value for that species at each stage of growth. If you can't tell one species of grass from another, ask your state extension specialist for help.

Hay is for Horses

Hay should be the primary forage for horses in wintertime, or year round for stabled horses with limited or no access to grazing. Hay is preserved pasture plants that have been dried to less than 20 percent moisture content. As a general rule, fresh plants in the pasture are 14 to 20 percent dry matter. As hay, the same plants offer 75 to 80 percent dry matter. When you compare feed values, pasture plants offer about one-quarter the feed value of hay, due to the higher water content.

Haymaking is a fine art and a science. It takes good-quality grass cut at the right time to produce good hay. Hay quality depends on the skill of the farmer, cooperation from the weather, and the timing of the cutting. The optimal cutting period is at the pre-bloom stage of growth, just before the flowers form. Once the grass is cut, the quality of the resulting hay depends on the speed of drying, how long the grass spent lying in the field, and whether or not it was rained on.

Haymaking can only preserve the quality that is present in the grass at the time of haymaking. If the grass is poor quality, full of weeds, and too mature, then making it into hay will not improve the feed quality and in most cases will actually decrease nutritional value.

HOW GRASS PLANTS GROW

Grass plants produce new growth during the spring. The cell walls of the new leaves contain cellulose, which provides stability. To strengthen the stems so that they can provide support for the flowers and leaves, the walls of the cells are increasingly fortified with lignin. As the plant matures the number of strong stems increases, and thus it contains more and more lignin. By the time the plant has produced seeds, its life cycle is nearly over. At this point it is mostly lignin with cellulose, with a small amount of green area for photosynthesis.

Making Hay

Hay is usually named after the legume or grass that is present in the highest percentage. Thus, timothy hay is produced from timothy grass. Lespedeza hay is made from the legume lespedeza. Fescue hay is made from fescue, and so on. Mixed grass hay is a combination (which may or may not be identified). The feed quality of the final product depends not only on the quality of the original plant and the stage of development the plant was at when cut, but also on how well the hay was dried and stored after cutting.

As grass plants grow during the spring, cellulose and then indigestible lignin are layered in the developing leaves and stems; eventually the plant will produce flowers and then seeds, completing its life cycle. It will then die back, leaving the lignin-filled skeleton of stalks and leaves.

In order to make good hay, the farmer must catch the grass at just the right moment in its lifecycle, when it has developed maximal leaves and stalks but before it has produced seeds. Hay made

In order to make good hay, the farmer must catch the grass at just the right moment in its lifecycle, when it has developed maximal leaves and stalks but before it has produced seeds. The optimal cutting period for hay is at the pre-bloom stage of growth, just before the flowers form.

from grass that has gone to seed will contain plenty of stalks and lignified leaves, but will offer very little nutritional value. Hay made too early in the plant's life, on the other hand, will have a high moisture content and will tend to crumble easily when dried, although it will retain a high level of digestible nutrients. But grass cut too early will be hard to dry properly, and the dried leaves will easily crumble and drop off as dust, known as leaf drop. Because most of the feed value of the plant lies in the leaves, significant leaf drop means a significant loss of nutritive value. This is one of the main causes of nutrient loss in hay during storage. Thus, good hay-making is a balance between too much lignin (grass too mature) and too little (grass too young).

In a field containing mixed grasses, not all the plants will flower at the same time. Generally in a mixed pasture, some grasses will be flowering, some will have gone to seed, and some will still be in the pre-flowering state. Making hay from mixed grasses is a hit or miss exercise, and one can never be sure when the mixture is at optimal nutritional status. The task is much easier when all the plants are of the same species, such as timothy or orchard grass. If all the plants were planted at the same time and all have a similar life cycle, the chances increase that all plants are at the same stage of development. The better quality hays are usually made from specifically grown plants, rather than a mixed stand of unknown composition.

Assuming that the quality of the plants being harvested is good, drying is the most important stage of the process for ensuring the subsequent quality of the hay. If hay does not dry quickly enough, then mold can develop, and the hay will be toxic to horses. (See Chapter 8.) To help speed the drying process, many farmers use a process called mower conditioning. Mower-conditioners crush the plant stems as they cut, allowing the plant to dry faster. This is especially important when making hay from legumes like alfalfa, since they tend to have thicker stalks, which take longer to dry.

Unfortunately, in speeding up the drying process, the mower-conditioner also allows the hay to deteriorate faster. While it is often better made, it will deteriorate faster when stored in the barn due to the exposure of the stalks to air, bacteria, and molds. Hay that has deteriorated is lower in feed value in terms of the vitamin content and the protein level. Such hay will require that concentrates be added to the diet to ensure adequate nutrition. Hay that has mold growth will cause respiratory problems, among other things, and should not be fed.

If the hay gets rained on after cutting, it will of course take longer to dry out and may become infected with mold. The younger the plants are at cutting and the higher the nutritive value of the plants, the faster molds will move in. If the grass is cut after flowering when there is minimal nutritive value, then the drying period is not quite as critical because molds will move in more slowly due to the lower feed value. Of course, the horses don't derive much nutritional benefit from such hay either, but at least they won't develop an allergy to mold spores and develop chronic obstructive pulmonary disease (COPD), or "hay-cough". See Chapter 8 for more on COPD.

Healthy Hay

Forages provide the greatest variation in feed values of all the available feedstuffs. There is considerable variation in the feed value of hay depending on how well the grass was fertilized and how young it was when cut. Values provided by the tables in the appendix are average values only; the values in specific cuttings of hay, either made or bought, can vary widely. If you are serious about learning the specific feed value of a particular batch of hay, you will need to have it analyzed. This can be done through your state extension office or a commercial lab. Most dairy farmers have their hay analyzed and then balance the rations to match the hay exactly. If you have dairy farmers in your area, ask one of them for the name and address of a commercial lab, or your state extension office can supply a list.

Grass hays have a medium-to-low protein content; the exact amount depends on what stage they were at in their life cycle when the hay was made. Grass hays are usually made high in fiber to allow for easier drying and storage, so grass hays tend to provide lower protein but more fiber. Horses tend to prefer stalky plants in their hay and thus prefer hay made from grasses such as orchard grass and timothy to the softer, leafier meadow grasses such as brome, redtop, or fescue.

Most horses love the taste of alfalfa, but alfalfa tends to have a protein content that's excessive for most adult, non-working horses. However, alfalfa is a good choice for broodmares and young stock. It can provide up to 50 percent of their hay ration; more than that will contribute too much protein and increase urine output. Alfalfa should be fed with caution and in limited amounts to other horses. A flake a day as a treat is enough for most, but be sure to provide plenty of stalky grass hay as the main ingredient of the ration.

Pregnant mares should not be fed fescue hay, which leads to problems with endophyte toxicity. (See Chapter 8 under feed toxins.)

Hay Storage

Hay for horses should be stored off the ground and under cover to protect it from precipitation and dampness, and it should be put up for storage only when completely dry. Horses are *very sensitive* to mold toxins in any feed, and hay is particularly susceptible to mold. Improper storage or putting the hay up while its damp will result in mold growth and related health problems in the horses that eat it. Over time, continual exposure to molds will cause allergies in horses and result in the horse losing up to three-quarters of its functioning lung surface. When buying horse hay, above all make sure it is *clean*. There is no such thing as mold-free hay, but mold content of hay intended for horses should be minimal. (See Chapter 6 for more information on storing hay and other feed.)

Clean and Green

Good hay should be bright in color and crisp. Bales of grass hay should weigh between 30 and 50 pounds; legume hay will weigh more. Avoid hays that are dark in color or brownish or that have visible white growths of mold. If the hay bales are hot to the touch, they are fermenting and should never be stacked for storage area; they may heat up to the point of combustion and cause a potentially serious fire.

Hay should separate easily when lifted up or shaken. Hay that produces a white cloud of mold spores when shaken or has a sharp, moldy smell **should not be fed.** If you see a white or gray fuzz over the plant stalks and leaves that tends to "glue" the hay stalks together, you are seeing (and smelling) mold: discard the hay. Give it to a cattle farmer or landscaper for mulch, and don't even store it near the horses.

The cleanliness of your hay is more important to horses than actual feed value. Most horses get plenty of nutrition from the grain and concentrates they are fed. So if your only choice is between high-feed-value hay with mold in it and low-feed-value hay with little mold, then pick the latter. The best, of course, is high-quality hay with little or no mold.

LEARN TO IDENTIFY GOOD HAY

Here's what you need to know to select quality hay that will keep your horse in bloom. The hay you buy to store in your hay barn should:

1. Be as free as possible from mold. Avoid hay with any moldy smell. Open a bale to check. Look for clouds of mold puffing up when hay is shaken. Reject any bales you suspect of containing mold.

2. Be crisp and clear in color. The exact color depends on the grass or legume harvested. The outside of any bales that have been exposed to air might be brownish, but the inside hay should be greeny gold. Good hay is rarely black, dark brown, or medium brown in color, with the exception of some clover and lespedeza hays, which tend to go brown in storage but are fine in nutritive quality. With all legume hays, be especially wary of mold. Molds love legumes.

3. Be palatable. This means the horses eat it willingly and clean up all they are given. The only place hay can benefit the horse is in its stomach.

4. Contain minimal weed content, particularly minimal thistle content. Horses won't eat hay with a lot of thistle and other weeds. If they don't eat it, it has no value.

5. Contain individual grass stalks or legume plants that are clearly distinguishable, not all crushed together into an impenetrable mass. The latter is a sign of hay that was baled too wet and usually indicates high mold content.

Above all, if a horse won't eat a batch of hay, trust the animal's assessment that something is seriously wrong with that hay and replace it with palatable hay.

Choose the best hay you can afford. Most horses will greedily eat good hay and very few will reject hay unless there is a problem. Feeding good hay can make quite a difference to your feed bills and to your horse's appearance by the end of the winter. Wasted hay and vet bills for sick horses will soon eliminate any savings you might think you make by buying poor-quality hay. If horses consistently reject hay, it means that the hay is not of good enough quality. If a horse won't eat the hay, don't just leave it in the stall "until he learns to clean it up." It won't happen! The horse will get sick or lose weight rather than eat it. If a horse rejects the hay, remove it and replace it with fresh and, hopefully, better hay.

Hay in Winter

It's important to provide plenty of hay to horses in the winter. Hay helps them stay warm and assists in preventing colic and other digestive upsets. As a rough guideline, a 1,200-pound horse should eat a minimum of half up to a full bale (20 to 40 pounds) of hay a day. So when you buy your hay, calculate for at least half a bale per horse per day for the five to six winter months. That adds up to roughly 75 to 100 bales per horse for half of the year, minimum.

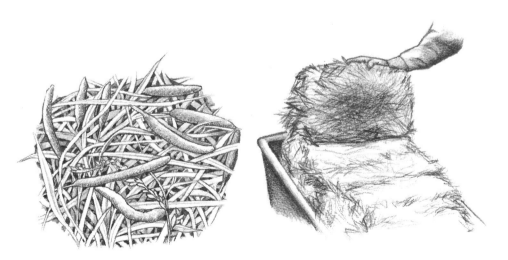

In good-quality hay you can clearly distinguish the individual stalks of grass or legume plants.

This is a maintenance ration. If hay is in short supply or only poor hay is available, buy enough to supply the minimum forage/fiber needs; the extra nutritive needs can be met by the grain portion of the ration.

Silage and Haylage

Silage is fodder conserved by the process of anaerobic fermentation. Silage is very popular in Europe, but is much less common in North America. The longer sunlight hours and higher temperatures in North America make it easier to dry hay, and there is generally less of a problem with high mold content in American hay and consequently less need for preservation through ensiling. Silage-making takes a degree of expertise that is generally less common in North America.

Silage replaces hay in the ration. It is a source of digestible fiber and can be an excellent feed for horses. The protein content depends on the grass it was made from. Horses do take some time to get used to the taste and smell of silage, but once they do, they usually enjoy it. It is particularly useful for horses with Chronic Obstructive Pulmonary Disease (COPD — see Chapter 8) or other hay allergies. Silage has a higher water content than hay (around 60 percent dry matter as opposed to the 85 percent dry matter in hay), so feed slightly more in order to meet the fiber requirements.

Silage can be produced from a number of different forages, but for horses, grass is most common. Horses can eat well-made corn silage and usually do well on it, though this is less common. Fermentation takes place in various ways. In one method, grass is piled in a huge "clamp" or pit and is compressed to exclude all oxygen. Another approach encloses round bales in plastic bags that are sealed against oxygen; long tunnels of plastic are also used. Again, the grass is compressed to exclude air and the plastic is sealed to keep the air out. Smaller plastic bags that ferment one small bale is the silage method most often used for horse silages.

Small bale silage — if well made and kept oxygen-free — is an excellent forage feed for horses. In Europe, a highly compressed form of grass silage is packaged in small plastic bags. The product is called variously Horsehage, or Propack, or Haylage, depending on the manufacturer. This small bag silage is usually drier (high in dry matter) and is more suitable for horses than clamp or tower silage, plus it is a lot easier to handle and feed. The silage produced in the big silos is usually wetter and smellier and requires a tractor with a front-end loader to move it. Europeans also make silage by round baling semi-dried grass and putting the entire round bale into a giant, sealed plastic bag. Big bale silage is cheaper to buy, but is harder to manage and less efficient to feed.

Also, unless great care is taken with the ensiling process, it can be a source of botulism. The botulism originates in the bodies of small mammals who get accidentally caught up in the round bale and become ensiled along with the grass. The horse will eat the small mammal along with the grass, and so great care needs to taken to sort through round bale silage prior to feeding to remove any small bodies. If planning to feed big bale silage, it may well be worthwhile vaccinating the horses against botulism.

As you should now fully realize, horses are more sensitive to mold than cattle are, and you must take care to provide only reliable, clean silage. Eliminate the moldy clumps that sometimes develop if not all the oxygen has been excluded or where there is an air leak.

Chopped Hay Options

Several companies, including Dengie and Triple Crown, offer a chopped hay product that is compressed into bags. The hay is cut to a shorter length than typical baled hay and often sprayed with a little molasses to minimize dust and increase palatability. Chopped hay products can be used to increase the amount of fiber in a concentrate ration or to give a horse something to eat at feed times besides a concentrate. They can also be used to augment supplies when hay is in short supply or be fed when you're away from home for a period of time to ensure consistent forage.

Alfalfa cubes

THE BEST WAY TO FEED ALFALFA CUBES

The dried squares of alfalfa called alfalfa cubes are best fed either by wetting them down or soaking. If fed dry to a horse that does not chew well or who eats them too fast, chunks of the dried cubes can cause the horse to choke.

To soak alfalfa cubes, put them into a tub or bucket, cover with water, and allow to sit for 10 to 20 minutes. Once the cubes have soaked up enough water, they should be mushy, with no discernable lumps. Feed the soaked cubes right away. Any that the horse has not eaten in two to four hours should be discarded because once wet, the cubes will spoil quickly.

If your horse begins to choke, call a vet. While waiting for the vet, remove all feed and hay and encourage the horse to drop its head low to facilitate drainage of saliva out of the nostrils and keep it from draining into the lungs. If you can see the blockage as a lump in the esophagus, try to massage the esophagus to see if you can move or break up the blockage (see Chapter 8).

Another option is alfalfa cubes or pellets, made from the cut, dried, and ground plant. They usually have a similar nutritional content to alfalfa hay and can be used to augment fiber in the ration. As they are less bulky than baled hay, they can be stored more easily and are convenient to handle. Dried alfalfa cubes can contribute a very valuable source of fiber to a ration for those horses who cannot eat hay or whose hay supplies are limited. However, due to the grinding process, little or no long fiber remains for the horse to chew. Therefore, alfalfa cubes may not satisfy the chewing needs of the horse. When alfalfa cubes are fed as a substitute for hay, the amount fed needs to be balanced into the ration (see Chapter 4).

If you must supply a fiber substitute for hay, offer a mixture of several other fiber sources as well as alfalfa cubes, which provide excessive protein if used alone. Examples are chopped grass, sugar beet pulp, or soy hulls. There has recently been a trend to produce ground grass products, as well as alfalfa; grasses are lower in protein and higher in fiber than alfalfa and may be better for the horse's digestive system.

All About Concentrates

Concentrates are grain-based feeds that are low in fiber and provide a higher digestible energy content than typical forage. That means that they offer a higher level of simple carbohydrates and sometimes a higher level of protein. Concentrates can include traditional cereals, such as oats, barley, corn (maize), and, in some cases, grains like rye, rice, and wheat.

The concentrate category also includes the commercial blends and pellets produced by various feed companies. These are usually blends of grains and by-products, fortified with vitamins and minerals. The benefit of commercial mixes is that because they offer a blend of different ingredients designed to meet specific nutritional requirements, they are less likely to be short in specific nutrients.

While whole grains can be beneficial, some are deficient in valuable nutrients; if you are feeding only one type of grain, there is a risk that necessary nutrients may be missing. This is less of a concern if you feed a commercial mix or blend. If you are feeding only whole grains, take care to balance the ration and to include an appropriate vitamin/mineral supplement. Nutritional values for various grains are provided in Table 3 in the Appendix.

Keep in mind that there is no such thing as the perfect grain; rations need to be fed and balanced as a whole, including the contributions of hay and pasture and taking into account the activity level and other special needs of the horse. See Chapter 4 for more details.

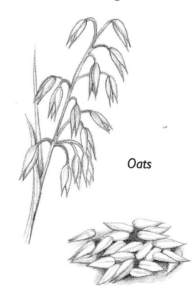

Oats

Whole Grains

Oats. Because they are high in fiber and are less likely to form a solid mass in the GI tract that could lead to an impaction colic, oats *(Avena sativa)* have historically been the grain of choice for horses. However, oats do not offer any other special nutritional value compared with other cereal grains. Most oat varieties contain around 1.3 Mcal per pound, with 12 percent protein and 11 percent fiber. You can easily incorporate oats into the horse's ration as long as you calculate the overall balance and address the mineral deficiencies. Like many cereal grains, oats are low in calcium and high in phosphorus.

The hull of the oat grain needs to be cracked or broken open to provide access to the digestive enzymes. You can purchase oats in a variety of different forms, ranging from whole oats (the least processed) through cracked, rolled, clipped, crimped, and ground versions (each term describes the particular process for breaking open the hull). The hull protects the grain from mold and insects, so the various hull-cracking processes reduce the amount of time that cracked oat grains can be stored before they deteriorate.

Recently, a naked or hull-less oat has been developed; this variety has much less fiber in its seed coat and is higher in energy density. Hull-less oats provide around 1.7 Mcal per pound, around 18 percent crude protein, and only 2.4 percent fiber. The diminished fiber in the hull-less oats means that the safety margin that the fiber in traditional oats afforded is absent. As with other grains without shells, like corn, wheat grain, sorghum, or rye, the danger of overfeeding hull-less oats must be avoided.

Corn. Corn, or maize *(Zea mays),* is a common horse feed. Slightly less palatable than oats, corn has a higher energy density than oats due to the lower fiber content of the hull. Corn contains 1.5 Mcal per pound, around 9 percent protein and 2.2 percent fiber. Be aware that corn is prone to problems with mold, resulting in the diseases equine leukoencephalomalacia and less often aflatoxicosis (see Chapter 8).

Because of the lower fiber content of corn, it is easy to overfeed, contributing to overweight or over-exuberant horses. Corn has a reputation for making horses "hot." To avoid this scenario, feed it according to the energy needs of the horse. If fed in suitable amounts, corn is as safe as any other grain. To reduce its calorie value, feed less of it.

Corn

Corn may be fed whole or processed. If the corn grains are processed and cooked, as in flaked or micronized versions, the starch is better digested in the small intestine, and less of the starch will reach the hind-gut, which is ideal because starch in the hind-gut can contribute undesirable levels of fermentation (see Chapter 1).

Barley. Barley *(Hordeum vulgare)* has the distinction of being the first grain ever domesticated by man. It is also the grain that is grown in the widest geographical area. Barley is a suitable feed for horses, usually fed either rolled, crimped, or cooked, as in flaked versions. Cooking definitely improves both the digestibility and palatability of the grain. Except for cooking, it is questionable whether other processing actually improves digestibility. Barley is less palatable than either oats or corn and is usually incorporated into mixed feeds that are sweetened with molasses, although some horses will eat it willingly.

Of the barley grown in the United States, about 50 percent is used for animal feed, 25 percent is used for alcohol production, and the rest is exported. Barley has a hull, as do oats, and its fiber value is between oats and the hull-less grains such as corn. Barley contains 1.5 Mcal per pound and around 12 percent crude protein and 5 percent fiber.

Distiller's grains and brewer's grains are barley by-products. Once barley has been ground and fermented to make beer (by brewers) or alcohol (by distillers), the bulk of the starch is fermented out. What remains is high in protein and low in digestible energy. Distiller's grains and brewer's grains are typically added as protein supplements to mixed feeds.

Barley

Wheat. Wheat *(Triticum aestivum)* is generally too expensive to use for animal feed, and by far the bulk of what is produced becomes human food. However, by-products like wheat bran and middlings — the hulls of the wheat grain removed to produce white flour — of wheat processed for human food are often incorporated in mixed feeds.

The high levels of a protein called gluten in wheat present a problem with using whole wheat for horse feed. Gluten, the protein that provides the "stickiness" in wheat flour that is prized by bakers, may lead to impaction colic. But once cooked, the gluten is denatured and becomes safe to feed. Thus, the wheat middlings (the portion just inside the hull, usually a mixture of hull and some flour) that are commonly incorporated into pellets are safe, because the pellets themselves are cooked at high pressure.

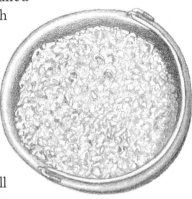

Wheat bran

Bran, the outermost husk of the wheat, is another by-product of wheat milling. This high-fiber feed has long been used to provide a low-calorie, high-fiber dinner for horses on rest days or sick days. However, bran has fallen out of favor in recent years. It is high in phosphorus and must have calcium added to balance the minerals. Additionally, bran contains compounds that bind calcium and render it unavailable during digestion. However, wheat bran is still added to mixed feeds as a fiber source. Bran was traditionally used as a laxative feed, but there is no evidence that it increases the rate of digesta passage through the equine GI tract. Calcium must be added to counterbalance high phosphorus levels. Nutritionally, wheat grain contains 1.55 Mcal per pound, 13 percent crude protein and around 3 percent fiber.

Rye. Rye *(Secale cereale)* grows in poor soil and cold weather and is more common in northern climates. It is not a customary feed grain for horses and is more typically cultivated for grazing or hay, although occasionally the grain is harvested for feed.

Rye grain supplies 1.5 Mcal per pound, 12 percent crude protein, and 2.2 percent fiber. The grains are very small and hard and need to be processed by grinding or cracking to allow digestion. Rye is fairly unpalatable as a grain and should only comprise one-third of the grain portion of a blend. However, rye hay is palatable and makes a useful forage for horses, with a feed value very similar to good grass hay (0.75 Mcal per pound, 8 percent protein, and plenty of fiber). In humid, hot climates, rye is very prone to a fungus called ergot that causes mycotoxin poisoning. (See Chapter 8.) Care must be taken to ensure there is no ergot in either rye grain or rye hay.

Rice. Rice *(Oryza sativa)* is largely used for human food. As with wheat, rice by-products may be added to animal feeds. When rice is processed for human food, the outer husk and seed coat, which contain the bulk of the fiber, are removed. The bran (the portion just inside the hulls that is ground off to produce white rice) contains a considerable level of fat (around 20 percent). However, it is very low in calcium and, due to the high fat content, spoils easily. However, if the bran is ground, balanced with added calcium, and stabilized by the addition of natural tocopherols (vitamin E), it becomes a very useful high-fat feed for horses. Sold as "Stabilized Rice Bran," it is now much more readily available than in the past. The fat in rice bran is extracted and sold as the oil gamma oryzanol. Gamma oryzanol is reported to have muscle-building properties, but this is entirely anecdotal and may be attributed to the high level of essential fatty acids it contains. If you feed rice bran, there is no need to add gamma oryzanol as the fats are identical.

Rice contains 1.5 Mcal per pound, 9 percent crude protein, and around 9 percent fiber (before polishing).

Grain Sorghum (Milo). The family of sorghum varieties *(Sorghum vulgare)* includes grasses, grain, broom corn, and syrup sorghums. The grasses include such species as Johnson grass and Sudan grass, which in some parts of the world are used as pasture or hays or for haylages. The syrup comes from the sorgo variety and broom corn is used for broom making. Although green sorghums and wild sorghums can be high in cyanide and prussic acid and should not be grazed, the varieties appropriate for pasture and hays are specially bred to not produce cyanides.

Cyanide toxicosis is not a problem with grain sorghums, which are used primarily for animal feed in North America and for human food in Africa and Asia. The modern varieties of grain sorghum are derived from a milo-kafir cross, sometimes referred to as milo. The grain comes in several different varieties, some of which contain high levels of tannic acid. The tannins make them unpalatable, and, as a general rule, the color of the grain can indicate how much tannin they contain. The darker the grain, the more tannin is present. Light yellow or pale sorghums can be fine for horses. Because sorghum is a small, hard grain, it needs to be processed before feeding to animals. As it is fairly unpalatable on its own, it is usually incorporated in grain mixes that can be sweetened with molasses. Nutritionally, grain sorghum contains 1.45 Mcal per pound, 11.5 percent crude protein, and around 2.6 percent fiber.

For a full comparison of grain values refer to Table 3 in the Appendix.

Other Sources of Fiber

Here are some other ways of introducing fiber into a horse's diet.

Sugar beet pulp. The dried, fibrous remains left after the sugar has been extracted from sugar beets provides a beneficial high fiber, low sugar feed for horses. Beet pulp usually comes either as pellets or loose shreds. The pellets have been compressed and need to be soaked before feeding; the shredded form does not require soaking. Due to its low sugar content, sugar beet pulp sometimes has molasses added to increase palatability.

Beet pulp has an energy value of 1.2 Mcal per pound dry weight, 10 percent crude protein, and about 20 percent fiber and is higher in calcium than phosphorus. It is a common form of added fiber in high fiber feeds such as senior feeds and in complete pellets or mixes. (Complete mixes are those designed to replace hay as well as grain.)

When incorporating sugar beet pulp pellets in a balanced ration, be sure to weigh the pellets dry. Calculate based on dry weight, then add enough water to ensure that all the pellets disintegrate.

Straw. Straw, the stalks of cereal plants left after harvest, is traditionally used as bedding, but many horses find it palatable, especially oat straw. Wheat and barley straw are often too ligneous to use as feed and have spicules or awns that prick the mouth. Straw can be used to provide fiber if hay is scarce. The feed value of straw is very low, about 0.7 Mcal per pound dry weight and 4 percent crude protein, but provides a whopping 40 percent fiber. If you use straw

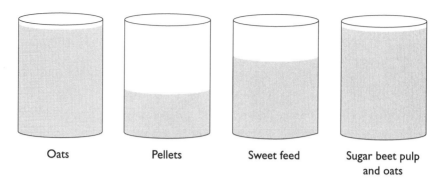

| Oats | Pellets | Sweet feed | Sugar beet pulp and oats |

Two pounds of grain can have very different density, depending on the feed.

as a fiber supply, increase the nutrient density in the concentrate portion to make up for the low protein and lack of vitamins.

Stover. The post-harvest stalks and remains of corn or sorghum, often left in the field, are known as stover. Animals were traditionally turned out on fields after harvest to eat what they would. Stover can provide a small amount of energy, but there is a risk of mycotoxicosis from the mold that grows on corn ears and leaves. Stover is a better feed for ruminants like cattle than for horses.

Hulls. The outer coating of many grains or seeds, hulls from oats, soy, almonds, sunflowers, or rice may be included in commercial feeds. Due to the likelihood of mouth irritation, some, like rice hulls, cannot be fed unless ground first. Since most hulls are high in fiber and fairly unpalatable, they are more commonly found in commercial blends and wetted with liquid molasses to make them less dusty and better tasting. Soy hulls are beginning to be considered an acceptable feed for horses. They contain 0.8 Mcal per pound dry matter, 12 percent crude protein, and 34 percent fiber, and are higher in calcium than phosphorus.

Citrus pulp and apple pomace. In parts of North America where fruit is grown and processed for juice or jellies, citrus pulp and apple pulp or pomace are produced as by-products. Citrus pulp is nutritionally similar to sugar beet pulp, but has a bitter taste and is very unpalatable to horses. A small amount can be incorporated into pellets or mixed feeds. Fruit pomaces are treated with limestone (calcium carbonate) during processing, so citrus pulp and pomaces are generally high in calcium.

About Molasses

Molasses is a thick, dark-colored liquid (occasionally a solid) produced from cane, beet, sorghum, corn, citrus, or wood. It is primarily sugar. Cane and beet molasses are the types most commonly fed to horses. Molasses is frequently added to commercial grain mixes and feeds. When molasses coats the grain or mix and can be seen and smelled, this characterizes the blends known as "sweet feeds." Generally in pelleted feeds, which contain less molasses, molasses is used as a binder.

Most horses will readily consume molasses and can develop a craving for the sugar. Many misbehaviors, both under saddle and in the barn, can be remedied by simply replacing sweet feed with a suitably balanced and nutritious ration of primarily whole grains.

Molasses contains 1.6 Mcal per pound dry weight (liquid molasses is about 70 percent dry matter) and 4 percent crude protein. It contains virtually no vitamins or fat. The calcium level in molasses is 1 percent higher than the phosphorus (0.1 percent).

Commercial Blends

Most horses in North America are fed some kind of commercial blend of grains, grain by-products, and other special additives. Concentrate mixes must contain an optimal amount of fiber, because horses do not flourish on mixes that contain too little fiber. In commercial mixes, roughage is often provided by some kind of cereal by-product, typically the remains left after the cereal has been processed for human consumption. These by-products can include such things as the hulls (outer shells) of oats, barley, almonds, peanuts, soybeans, cottonseed, rice, or sunflower seeds. Or the fiber can come from the pulp by-product from processing soybeans, sugar beets, apples, citrus fruits, or tomatoes. Many of these by-products are useful sources of fiber for the horse.

Some specialized commercial mixes, such as those for brood mares or growing foals, may require additional protein supplements and a higher level of minerals to meet their higher nutritional requirements. (See Chapter 5 for more information regarding specialized feeding.)

Mixes formulated for senior horses usually contain fermentable fiber — the types that are digested in the hind-gut, such as sugar beet pulp or soy hulls. Older horses often cannot chew hay efficiently, and the mixes made for them will supply more fiber in a form that's easier to chew. The mix will also be fortified with extra protein and minerals.

It always pays to read the labels on the feed mix bags carefully. The ingredients are usually listed in the order of greatest to least quantities. Remember that the protein value provided is for crude protein and does not address the question of protein quality. Things like soybean meal, alfalfa meal, cottonseed meal, and peanut meal represent protein sources.

Protein: What and Why

Protein supplements are only required when the ration as a whole is deficient in protein, as is likely if the horse is receiving poor quality hay, if there is little or no pasture, or if straw is being used to increase fiber in the diet. If you are feeding a commercial mix, then you probably don't need additional protein. But do read the label to learn the source of the protein it provides.

The main concern with high protein diets is the characteristic high urine output; the excess ammonia produced can make the stall an unpleasant place for humans and horses, as well as leading to respiratory problems in the horse. In addition, high protein diets can increase metabolism, making it difficult for the horse to cool down in hot weather. An inability to reduce body heat can be a serious problem in hot climates.

Most cereal grains provide ample protein quantity but low protein quality. If you are feeding only whole grains, address the quality issue by providing a suitable protein supplement, either animal-based or high-grade plant proteins — your best option.

Although animal protein is usually higher in the essential amino acids, especially lysine, and hence higher in nutritional quality than plant proteins, horses are true vegetarians and can be sensitive to animal products. Thus, animal-based protein supplements like milk powder, egg powder, and fish meal must only be used with great care and caution. **Meat or bone meal should not be fed to**

horses. Fish meal can be used as high-grade protein additive to improve poor quality grain or hay if the horse will eat it. Milk or egg powders offer a good source of very high quality protein in liquid feeds for horses recovering from starvation or surgery, but they need to be formulated and balanced by experts.

If you need to supplement your horse's protein levels, provide one of the higher grade plant proteins, such as oil seed meals. Oil seeds are seeds that are high in oil or fat. After the oils are extracted, the remaining meal is often incorporated as a protein source in animal feeds. Many oil seed meals, including linseed (flax), soybean, cottonseed, peanut, and canola, are added as protein sources to commercial blends of animal feeds. Such seeds naturally provide desirable amounts of protein; once the oil itself has been extracted, the protein proportion increases. Yeasts used in the brewing and distilling industries, such as brewer's yeast and distillers' grains, are also high in protein and can be incorporated in the diet as a protein supplement.

Sources of Fat

For some horses, including those that are insulin resistant or very hard working, it might be desirable to add additional calories in the form of fat rather than carbohydrates. Horses that need to gain weight or who misbehave on high-starch diets can benefit from additional fat in the diet. As you've learned, oil seeds contain a high level of readily digestible fat; they can be a very useful source of fat for horses. It is usually better to supplement fat by feeding oil seeds rather than the processed forms of fat. See Chapter 2 for more information on fats.

There are by-products of human food processing, like rice bran, that are also high in fat and useful in horse feeding. Additional fat can increase coat gloss, if the original diet is too low in fat. As a general rule, fat supplements for horses should be derived from vegetable sources rather than animal sources. Animal fats are usually highly processed saturated fats and do not contain as useful a mix of fatty acids as unprocessed plant sources do. Give horses things like whole flax, whole roast soy, or rice bran rather than commercial corn oil or fat supplements based on pork by-products or beef fat.

Corn oil is entirely fat, and therefore contains a lot of calories. Adding corn oil to the normal ration will supply calories and help the horse to gain weight. But commercial corn oil is highly processed, so it would be better to supply the same fat calories from a less processed source.

In Addition . . .

The need to supplement your horse's basic ration varies. This section will explore some common gaps that can be addressed by supplementation.

Feed Additives

Additives (as opposed to nutritional supplements) typically augment feeds to improve some aspect of feed handling or production rather than for nutritional enhancement. Additives like lignin help to bind pellets, and others help preserve feed. Others may benefit the animal in other ways, such as improving digestibility, absorbency, or palatability.

Zeolite, a bioavailable silica, offers proven benefits in improving bone absorbency. In several equine studies, the best results were observed when zeolite was fed at levels of around 2 percent by weight of feed.

Digestion enhancers include such ingredients as enzymes and chelating agents that improve mineral absorption. Buffers or acid neutralizers are assuming more important roles as the consequences of excess stomach acidity and its subsequent effects become better understood. It is becoming clear that many aberrant behaviors, from cribbing to bad temper at grooming and tacking up, may be due to stomach pain. In 2003, three papers on gastric pH and cribbing and incidence of ulcers and cribbing were presented at the Equine Nutrition and Physiology Society meeting. In all cases it was shown that horses with the most acidity in their stomachs displayed the most cribbing behavior. Antacids for horses are probably most effective if based on salts of magnesium and calcium. While there are a few on the market based on aluminum salts, and these are very effective at reducing acidity, the long-term effects of feeding aluminum have yet to be ascertained. (See Chapter 8 for more on cribbing.)

Probiotics, also known as bacteria inoculants, provide doses of desirable bacteria to enhance the population of bacteria in the hind-gut and improve microbial digestion. In any situation where the health of the hind-gut bacteria is compromised, probiotics (provided they supply the right species of bacteria) will be beneficial. The species of bacteria suitable for horses include species of lactobacillus *(L. acidophilus),* streptococcus, *(S. faecium),* and bacillus *(B. subtilis).* Consider supplementing with probiotics after oral medications, worming, strenuous travel, colic, overheating, or ingestion of toxic food. Provide probiotics only as needed, not every day. A daily dose for a week should provide enough to restore the natural population of the hind-gut. A probiotic is only as good as the number of live organisms it contains. Heat processing or pelleting will destroy them, so add live cultures at feeding time.

Yeast cultures supply the digestive bacteria with some nutrients and boost their metabolism. When giving probiotics, it's beneficial to also provide yeast cultures. Yeast cultures also provide a valuable supply of B vitamins, but their main benefit is in enhancing the activity of the hind-gut bacteria. Yeast cultures are beneficial on a daily basis.

Antibiotics are not routinely added to horse feeds. Some of the antibiotics that are commonly fed to cattle, pigs, and poultry are toxic to horses. For example the ionophore antibiotics lasolacid, monensin, and lincomycin will cause fatal arrhythmia, diarrhea, and colitis. It is important *not* to feed grains intended for other livestock to horses.

Mold inhibitors are sometimes added to feed to reduce incidence of mold growth. Horses are very sensitive to molds and to mycotoxins, toxins that come from molds. The most common mold inhibitor is propionic acid or its salts. Most other mold inhibitors are either pricey or ineffective in mixed feeds. The best way to prevent mold is to buy small amounts of feed and use it up in a reasonable time. Store the feed in a dry, cool place and avoid damp and heat, both of which encourage mold growth. (See Chapter 6.)

Antioxidants are often added to high-fat feeds to prevent oxidation (rancidity) of the fats. The most common antioxidants are ethoxyquin and BHT (butylated hydroxytoluene). Both are safe and have been used for years, but BHT occasionally has palatability problems. Vitamin E (tocopherol) can also be used as an antioxidant; the synthetic tocopherols can be effective at protecting the feed but cannot be absorbed into the body and hence cannot supply vitamin E to the body. The use of the natural tocopherols as preservatives is rare due to their high cost.

Electrolytes

The chemical definition of an electrolyte is a compound that dissociates in water to form positive and negative ions. However, in terms of horse feeding it usually refers to those ions and minerals lost in sweat. When horses work hard in warm or hot weather, their main opportunity to dispel excess heat is through sweat evaporation. In the process, they can lose a considerable quantity of ions. Because the ions in the sweat originate in blood plasma, muscle function is compromised if plasma levels drop. If levels of available ions in the blood drop too low, the horse cannot continue. In severe cases, it may become ill or even die.

The vital minerals present in sweat, in order of concentration, are potassium, sodium, chloride, magnesium, and phosphorus. Thus most electrolyte supplements aim to replenish these ions. The most important ones are sodium, chloride, potassium, and magnesium. Most forages provide ample potassium, so the mineral of most concern is sodium.

For most horses, the minerals provided in the feed should be sufficient to meet ordinary needs, but if the horse works hard, or the weather is hot and he sweats a lot, extra electrolytes should be provided. (See Chapter 2 for a couple of homemade formulas that will replenish lost electrolytes.)

Commercial Supplements

There are so many supplements on the market that offering a comprehensive list would more than fill up this book and quickly become outdated. But in general, before buying a commercial supplement for your horse, do a little research.

• What does the supplement really provide?
• Is there a bona-fide need for this nutrient by the horse?
• Check the ingredient list, not just the advertising claims.
• Discover what is actually in there, and what it is for; it should have sound science behind it, not a lot of hype.
• Don't select only by name. Names that sound similar do not mean that the two products supply the same nutrients.

One example of the sounds-like syndrome is Red-Cell, a product that supplies B vitamins and iron used for performance horses suspected of being anemic. Mega-Sel supplies selenium and vitamin E. These product names sound similar, but they supply totally different nutrients; you can't substitute one for the other!

If you are trying to solve a problem, don't try several different products at the same time. It's recommended that you use first one and then the other if the first doesn't produce the benefits you seek. If you give three at once and there is an improvement, you won't know which one is responsible for the improvement.

Allow the supplement a reasonable amount of time to work, and if it isn't producing the effect you want, stop using it and try another one. Most nutrients take at least two or three weeks to produce an effect, and some take longer. For instance, supplements for hoof growth can take up to six weeks before you see any actual improved growth. Be patient.

It's essential to keep accurate records, preferably by writing things down in a diary if you are measuring effects. Memory can be very inaccurate.

Are vitamin supplements really necessary? Most commercial feeds are fortified with added vitamins and minerals, so it is not always necessary to add more if you are using a good quality commercial mix. But if you are feeding mostly whole grains or only feeding small quantities of the blend, it may well be a good idea to add a good quality vitamin/mineral supplement.

In certain conditions (pregnancy, lactation, recovery from illness or stress, hard work, etc.) it may well pay off to supplement with extra vitamins and minerals. Refer back to Chapter 2 to review the roles of various nutrients and select your supplements according to the horse's particular needs.

Joint Supplements

What about offering joint supplements to horses with arthritis, navicular disease, or chronic injuries?

The special supplements sold for joints that contain chondroitin and glucosamine remain a bit controversial. There has been some research that shows that supplying the cartilage cells with glucosamine and chondroitin can slow degeneration and encourage regeneration, but most experiments have been conducted in a petri dish with cell cultures. So far, only one study on oral supplementation (done by Dr. Hilary Clayton at Michigan State University and published in 2003) showed a benefit from feeding oral glucosamine and chondroitin. If you decide to try these supplements, read the labels and do some math to learn how much of the active ingredients the product is supplying. The labels on many products are misleading, and there is huge variation in the amounts of chondroitin and glucosamine that the various products contain. Some offer appreciable amounts, while others contain very little.

It is a good idea to choose the products that have some testing and research behind them. From what little research we have to date, the supplement needs to supply glucosamine in both the hydrochloride (HCl) and the sulfate (SO_4) forms. It may be beneficial to look for chondroitin SO_4 and manganese, copper and zinc, plus antioxidants like vitamin C or alpha lipoic acid. Make sure the one you buy contains enough of the active ingredients to be effective, without a lot of filler like sugar. Look for a mixture that supplies 3,600mg of glucosamine and 1,200mg of chondroitin per day to be effective.

Herbal Cautions

Herbal preparations with all kinds of claims are offered on today's market. It's a mistake to think that herbal preparations are "drug free." A drug is defined as a pharmacologically active substance. Many of our most common and oldest medical drugs originally came from herbs or plants. Modern methods produce synthetic versions in the laboratory, but the active ingredients can still be obtained from botanical sources. Be careful when using herbal preparations, because all drugs, whether produced in plants or factories, can have side effects and sometimes produce negative interactions. Be aware that herbal preparations can, in the wrong dosage or if applied inappropriately, be harmful.

Herbal preparations often contain detectable compounds chemically similar to modern drugs. For example, the tranquilizer Valium is not permitted in horses competing in shows sanctioned by the United States Equestrian Federation, yet the herb valerian contains a compound that is chemically identical to Valium. If you give the herb valerian to your horse as a calmative, it will appear in the blood or urine assay as Valium. You will be disqualified from such a competition.

Very few herbal preparations can tell you the accurate dosage of the drugs they contain. Most are not adequately tested, and the plants can vary considerably in their drug concentrations. Thus herbal preparations can be useful, but must be given with caution and care. They are not risk or side-effect free!

A Bit About Treats

The question frequently arises: How often is it okay to include applesauce, fresh apples, carrots, corn husks or silk, or other "snacks" in a horse's diet?

The correct way to feed a treat is to hold your hand flat, with fingers and thumb together and treat on palm, or to drop the treat into a feed tub.

NATURAL? ORGANIC?

Don't confuse the terms "All-natural" and "Organic." Organic specifically means that the food has been produced without the use of synthetic pesticides, fertilizers, or chemical processing. "All-natural" indicates only that the feed or product exists in nature. Many things exist in nature, and not all of them are beneficial! So be aware when you read labels that organic and all-natural are not created equal.

Giving snacks in the feed is fine, even on a daily basis. Giving snacks by hand, however, should be limited, to minimize associated behavioral problems. Add fresh fruits and other snacks to the horse's bucket to avoid unwanted responses like grabbing and nipping.

You can give carrots, apples, sugar cubes, or even raw macaroni. If you remove the pits, horses love peaches and enjoy pears, too. Commercial treats are fine; some are even fortified with vitamins and minerals, so feel free to use them.

Feed-based Wormers?

There is no doubt that horses should be dewormed on a regular basis. Feeding a daily wormer means that the horse gets a low dose of the drug continuously, which in some cases can be better for the horse than a larger amount less often. However, a few horses do not do well on the daily wormers. If they react with episodes of colic, diarrhea, or loose stools, those horses should be put back on the larger oral dose every six weeks.

In Conclusion

Now that you have a basic understanding of what foods horses require to thrive and why a balanced ration is vital to health and well-being, the next question is: How do you design a feed program that meets all your horse's needs?

Learn all about it in the next chapter.

-4-

Designing a Balanced Feeding Program

I OFTEN HEAR THIS QUESTION FROM HORSE OWNERS: "How much should I be giving him?" It is tempting to answer, "Enough and no more!" But how much is enough? If you really want to know how to match your horse's specific needs to his daily intake, it is best to balance the ration.

Balancing a ration is a fairly time-consuming job and definitely not for the math-phobic. There are a number of computer programs that you can use, but because they are aimed at the professional nutritionist, they can be a little less than user-friendly. If you don't have access to a computer and you are not accustomed to ration calculations, either use a set of tables or make your best guess based on what you learn from labels and this book. Use the body score method described at the end of the chapter to assess your horse's condition and make adjustments.

In this book we will focus on the basic nutrient values of the most commonly fed grains and forages. If you want to learn more, the comprehensive method for calculating rations, along with tables of requirements for various minerals for different sizes and growth stages, is detailed in the National Research Council (NRC)

ORDER YOUR OWN COPY

To order a copy of *Nutrient Requirements of Horses,* write to the National Academies Press, 500 Fifth St, NW, Washington, DC 20001 Ask for the most up-to-date edition of *Nutrient Requirements of Horses,* ISBN # 0-309-0389-4.

publication *Nutrient Requirements of Horses.* The publication also provides tables for the average nutrient values of almost any feed you can think of.

Bear in mind that the NRC tables tend to provide minimum requirements rather than optimal. In the case of certain nutrients, I recommend that you increase the requirements above those given in the tables. This is especially pertinent for the minerals and vitamins. Refer back to Chapter 2 to refresh your memory about optimal nutrient levels. Or use the tables on Feed Requirements for Horses provided in the Appendix.

Also bear in mind that the values provided for the forages (grasses and the hays made from them) are averages. As discussed in Chapter 3, forages tend to vary widely in feed value depending on the soil they grew in, how much fertilizer was applied, the growth stage when the grass was cut, and the weather conditions when it was processed. If you are serious about knowing the specific nutrition values in the hay you are feeding, it is best to have your hay analyzed. Your local county extension office can tell you how to do this. To make up a hay sample, take a handful of hay from the center of at least six bales picked at random throughout the stack. Mix the samples up in a bag, shake well, pull out a handful or two, and place this into a sealable plastic bag. Send it to the state or a private laboratory. If you live in dairy country, most dairy farmers have their hay analyzed each year, so a farmer can tell you of a local lab, or show you how to sample hay.

If you are feeding commercial mixes or grains, you won't need to have it analyzed, because the feed company has already done that. The feed values are on the bag. If you are feeding homegrown grains, then they should be analyzed; take a sample from several bags, mix them together, place in a plastic bag and send it to the lab.

Most grains are analyzed by proximate or Weende analysis and most forages by Van Soest analysis. When you look on your grain bag the analysis you see will be a proximate analysis; the section below should help you understand what the values given mean.

Proximate Analysis Results

Once a proximate analysis on feed has been completed, the lab will send you a set of figures that include values like the CP (crude protein), NFE (nitrogen-free extract), EE (ether extract), crude fiber, and ash. Here's what those results indicate.

Crude Protein

Proteins contain roughly 16 percent nitrogen. The crude protein is calculated by measuring the amount of nitrogen and then multiplying by 6.25. This tends to be an overestimate, especially if the hay contains nitrates or urea. Thus the feed will never quite contain as much usable protein as it does crude protein, which is why you should allow a little leeway in the protein calculation. This is an issue only with homegrown feeds. Commercial feeds have been analyzed by the feed company. The feed value is written on the bag, or can be obtained by calling up the manufacturer and requesting it.

Nitrogen-Free Extract

The crude protein is measured and the amount is subtracted from the total weight of the feed to calculate the NFE, or nitrogen-free extract. This is a mixture of the carbohydrates, fats, and minerals. You need the energy value given in Mcal or the TDN (Total Digestible Nutrients). If the bag has the TDN value, then you need to convert it to Mcals. Remember from Chapter 2 that one pound TDN = 2.0 Mcal (or 1kg TDN = 4.4 Mcal).

Ether Extract

The ether extract is reported as crude fat. When a sample of the feed is mixed with ether, it dissolves out the fat. The ether/fat mix is removed and the ether evaporated; the remaining fat content can then be measured.

Crude Fiber

What is left after the ether extract is digested first in acid, then alkali provides the crude fiber value. The crude fiber contains both digestible and indigestible fiber portions. The problem with proximate analysis is that it does not distinguish between digestible and indigestible fiber. For that you will need a Van Soest analysis (see below).

Ash

If all organic matter is digested off, what remains is the ash value, or the minerals fraction. It is beyond the scope of this book to discuss the analysis of specific minerals. Just be aware that high ash values indicate a high mineral content.

Van Soest Analysis

For feeds that are high in fiber, like most forages, it is better to seek a detergent, or Van Soest, analysis, which measures the ADF (acid detergent fiber) and NDF (neutral detergent fiber) portions. (The NDF value indicates digestible fiber and the ADF the indigestible fiber.) This analysis is more useful for understanding the values that

---

IN BRIEF

Here are a few of the abbreviations that you will see frequently in this chapter.

Mcal = Megacalories
BW = bodyweight (in pounds, lbs or kilograms, kg)
TDN = total digestible nutrients

DM = dry matter
CP = crude protein
Mcal/lb = megacalories per pound
DE = digestible energy

your horse can utilize in his hay ration. All you need for ration calculations at this level is energy, protein, some minerals, and an idea of digestibility. Proximate analysis provides the first values, and Van Soest lets you know if the hay is digestible.

For people feeding insulin-resistant horses or those prone to founder, it is useful to request the Non-Structural Carbohydrates (NSC) value. The NSC will let you know if the hay is high in sugar and thus risky for your horse to eat. Ask the lab to analyze specifically for this factor, as many do not do so routinely.

Calculating Rations: The Basics

Calculating rations is a long, complicated task, so a simplified, easier method is offered here. This method is not as accurate, but can save you from some intense calculator use. The full method is primarily for professional nutritionists who are likely to use a computer program, which of course you can do, too, if you buy one.

A very good chapter on ration calculation is offered in the book *Feeding and Care of the Horse* by Lon D. Lewis. (See Appendix, Resources.) A set of equations for ration calculations also appears in the NRC book (see sidebar on page 96).

If you are feeding a diet of mostly whole grains or homegrown grains, it might be advisable to make at least a rough calculation and then adjust the diet as needed according to the horse's body score, explained at the end of this chapter.

Calculating Rations, Simplified

Based on values from the NRC tables, here is a rough method to calculate a ration. Grab a calculator! You will need either to remember a few figures or to jot them down on a card or in your notebook or diary.

If you are feeding racehorses, hardworking horses like three-day eventers, or seriously ill or debilitated horses, get help from a nutritionist. Calculating a feed ration for such horses is beyond the scope of this book.

First, Some Ground Rules

1. Nearly all calculations are based on bodyweight. Horses will consume roughly between 2 and 2.5 percent of their bodyweight per day in total dry matter (DM) intake. So you will need to know the approximate weight of the horse in question. Use a weight tape (most feed companies give them away) or a weighbridge if there is one near your home.

2. Remember: Forage (except in a very few special cases) is the most important element in the horse's diet. Only in special circumstances should horses receive less than 70 percent of their diet as forage. Only in very exceptional circumstances should one feed less than 50 percent. Most horse owners will use the 50 to 70 percent forage range.

For their own convenience, some people prefer to feed concentrates instead of forage. Hay is bulky, requires lots of storage space, and has to be fed in larger, frequent quantities. It is easier to go to the feed store and buy another bag of grain than to plan and organize good hay storage. If you can't or won't feed adequate quantities of hay, select concentrates with a high fiber inclusion, such as those based on sugar beet pulp or that include whole oats. Don't be surprised, however, if your horse responds to this reduced-forage diet with gastric distress. Your vet might want to stock up on her preferred colic treatments, because your horse will likely need them.

3. Monitor your horses and alter the diet as appropriate. Horses are individuals and should be fed as such. What suits Dobbin may or may not suit Smokey Joe, and vice versa. The tables are all based on average values, and your horse may or may not be "average."

Refer to the body score assessment at the end of this chapter for tips on monitoring your individual horse's condition.

4. Calculate all feeds by weight. This is important. Most horse people discuss feed in terms of volume, as in: "I give him a scoop of sweet feed and half a scoop of pellets daily." But sizes of scoops vary considerably. Make sure you know what is meant by "a scoop," what volume it is, and what "a scoop" of that feed weighs. Although a table of rough volume to weight conversions is located in the Appendix, it is best to weigh the actual feed you plan to use,

HOW MUCH?

I was advising a horse owner over the phone, and we had discussed the types of feed for her herd of young horses, which had been experiencing some growth problems. I kept saying that they needed X pounds of the concentrate, and she insisted on a translation into "coffee cans." "What kind of can?" I asked, "Oh, just a standard coffee can," she replied. To help us determine the accurate amount, I asked her to weigh the can when full of her particular brand of feed. The weights seemed quite off; either the feed was very dense or she was not weighing accurately. We floundered along for a time until I realized that I was assuming a 1-quart coffee can and she was using a gallon can!

because the table values can be off by up to 35 percent. An inaccuracy of that degree can make quite a difference.

5. Contrary to what is taught in most nutrition programs, relative to feeding your horse, breed does matter. European Warmbloods have been selected for feed efficiency and thriftiness, unlike Thoroughbreds and Quarter Horses. Horses of European extraction think that straw bedding is a buffet and will readily consume quantities. Pony breeds are even more thrifty, especially if they are less domesticated (e.g., semi-feral). Such ponies are more like mustangs than domestic horses and will pretty much eat anything that doesn't run away fast enough. There is a wonderful Thelwell cartoon about the New Forest Ponies in England "who live on a diet of fishpaste sandwiches and cakes stolen from tourists." So if you discover you have an "easy keeper" who gets fat just looking at hay, adjust quantities accordingly.

6. Take into account the horse's total environment; it will make a big difference whether the horse roams 20 acres of rough or lush pasture, or if it lives in a one-acre dirt lot with six others, with no access to grazing. It also matters if your hay is first cut (which usually means late cut, as in late in the life cycle of the plants) or second cut, which means cut later in the year but usually earlier in the life cycle of the plants. (See Chapter 3.) Refer to the tables for the feed values of various grasses and hays your particular horse encounters.

7. Few people have a clue about the quality of their hay. Learn as much as you can about the hay you feed; if it is grass hay, examine it for clues. More mature, stemmier hays provide a feed value that's lower by about 10 to 20 percent than is listed in the chart.

Remember, the chart is a guideline, not an absolute. Use the calculations to begin with and then use body score system to adjust as needed. The best plan of all is to have your hay analyzed so you know specifically what nutrients it supplies.

Basic Equine Requirements

Here are some basic guidelines and ballpark figures to keep in mind when establishing a feed program.

1. To supply appropriate energy needs, a horse requires approximately 1.5 Mcal DE/100 pounds bodyweight for maintenance.

2. Each hour of hard work (galloping, racing, polo) requires 1.8 Mcal DE/100 lbs BW/day — in addition to the maintenance requirement.

3. Moderate work (most English riding, including jumping) will require an extra 0.9 Mcal/100 lbs BW/day.

4. Each hour of light work (trail riding, western pleasure) demands 0.27 Mcal/100 lbs BW/day in addition to the maintenance requirement.

To learn energy values for a specific feed, either consult the feed label or look it up in the tables. A table that relates energy requirements to work is located in the Appendix.

The protein requirement is 40 × Mcal DE/day in grams. (Math tips: 453g = 1 lb.) For a 1,000-pound horse, 1,000/100 = 10 × .1.5 = 15 Mcal). So for the mythical 1,000–pound horse doing no work, the protein requirement is 40 × 15 Mcal = 600g/453g = 1.3 lb per day. For the same horse doing one hour of moderate work daily, the formula is 600g + (40 × 9.0 = 360) = 960g (2.1 lb).

Energy should always be balanced first and then protein calculated. Mineral needs can be met by feed and a commercial mix (refer to Chapter 2), either free access or added as a supplement.

If you have specific concerns, consult a set of nutrition tables to confirm the mineral values in the feed or supplements you provide.

Hay Requirements

Most hays, both grass and legume (if early cut), offer an energy content of around 1 Mcal/lb, so .015 × BW in pounds provides a rough estimate of the amount of hay required for maintenance.

Calculate to confirm that this amount is less than the 2 to 2.5 percent of bodyweight that the horse will consume. For example, our 1,000-pound horse will need to eat 15 to 16 pounds of quality, early-cut grass hay for maintenance. Two percent of 1,000 = 20 pounds, so the 16 pounds is well within the optimum intake for the animal. A grazing horse on good pasture will consume 4.4 pounds of grass per hour, of which 25 percent is dry matter, so the grazing horse will eat 1.1 pounds of dry matter in an hour. Grass contains roughly the same energy as good hay, so that 1.1 pounds will supply about 1.0 Mcals. Therefore, a grazing horse eating for 15 to 18 hours per day can consume enough grass to meet his energy needs.

If the hay is cut late (as most first-cut hays are) or otherwise of poor quality, then you need to increase the intake by roughly 20 percent: 16 lbs × 120 percent = 19.2 lbs, which is still within the normal intake range but getting close to the upper limits. To allow for wastage, you should feed a little extra, so 20 pounds of lesser quality hay is the amount that should be offered.

Protein content is the most variable factor in hays. Grass hays have around 10 percent if early cut and 7 percent if late cut. Legume hays contain around 20 percent.

FEED	DE MCAL/LB.	PERCENT PROTEIN	AMOUNT REQUIRED BY 1,000 LB HORSE	PROTEIN SUPPLIED HORSE FOR MAINTENANCE
Grass hay (early)	1.0	10 percent	16 lbs	726g/1.6lbs
Grass hay (late)	0.7	7 percent	20 lbs	635g/1.4lbs
Legume hay (early)	1.0	20 percent	16 lbs	1453g/3.2lbs
Legume hay (late)	0.8	16 percent	19 lbs	1380g/3.0lbs
Most grain feeds	1.7	As indicated on label	—	—

Most commercial sweet feeds and pellets contain around 1.7 Mcal/lb. The protein content should be listed on the bag and is usually identified as 10, 12, or 14 percent. Note that protein content is given in percentages, but you will need to calculate the actual amount in pounds or grams to confirm whether you are providing sufficient amounts.

We can see from our table that the horses on the grass hay receive adequate protein, and the horses on the legume hays get a good bit more than they need. To balance out the legume hay, feed less of it and more grass hay, or the high protein intake will result in excess urine and a stall that smells of ammonia.

Note we have only addressed protein quantity, not quality. If protein quality is a concern, such as when feeding young horses or those in hard work, it is best solved by feeding a high quality protein supplement containing enough essential amino acids, as discussed in detail in Chapters 2 and 3.

Practical Applications: Dobbin and Smokey Joe

Let's see how we would determine the best feeding program for two very different horses: Dobbin and Smokey Joe, who are both mature horses in good health. (Refer to Chapter 5 for specific age-related feeding issues.)

Feeding Dobbin

Dobbin is a mature gelding of mixed extraction, probably Quarter Horse or a Quarter Horse cross. You know or estimate his weight at 1,000 pounds. He lives in a pasture with three buddies and is ridden on weekends. He is at a good body score of 5 or 6 now, so there's no need for significant weight gain. (See sidebar on page 113.) For winter feeding (December through the end of March, in his part of the world), factor out the pasture as a feed source. For calculating spring and summer feeding, we will factor pasture back in.

For his energy requirement, multiply his bodyweight (BW) in pounds × .015 to derive Mcal of energy (expressed as DE). 1,000 × .015 = 15 Mcal.

Dobbin, a mature gelding, lives in a pasture with three buddies and is ridden on weekends.

For Dobbin's protein requirement, calculate $40 \times 15 = 600g$ divided by $453g = 1.32$ lbs of protein.

We now know that Dobbin requires approximately 15 Mcal of digestible energy (DE) and 1.3 pounds of protein per day for maintenance.

Early-cut grass hay provides 1.0 Mcal DE/lb and late-cut grass hay supplies 0.7–0.9 Mcal DE/lb. To receive the 15 Mcal/day he needs, Dobbin should get 14 to 16 pounds of early-cut or 18 to 21 pounds of late-cut grass hay per day. At his bodyweight, he will easily consume 20-plus pounds, so he will do fine on free choice hay and may even gain weight.

Choose one good quality vitamin/mineral supplement that covers all the bases. There are a lot of them on the market and most of the reputable ones are fine. You can give him a small handful of grain in a bucket on a regular basis — not to meet nutritive needs, but so that you see him regularly and you can mix in the mineral and vitamin supplement he gets. Choose a high fiber, low carbohydrate grain so he does not get too fat. Remember to deduct the weight in grain you give him from his hay intake. That is, if you give Dobbin 1 pound of grain, feed 1 pound less of the hay.

Is he getting enough protein? He needs 1.3 pounds daily. Since early-cut grass hays contain approximately 10 percent protein and late-cut 7.0 percent, 15 pounds of early-cut hay will provide 1.5 pounds of protein, which is ample. Twenty pounds of late-cut hay will provide 1.4 pounds of protein. Since he's already close to the maximum quantity he will readily consume, Dobbin needs a higher-quality hay.

You might add in a little alfalfa or a concentrate ration to compensate for the protein shortfall in the late-cut hay. One good way to do this is by using a balancer pellet: that is, a pellet that is especially high in protein, vitamins, and minerals. Feed in very small quantities, such as a pound or two a day to meet his nutritional needs without oversupplying energy.

If you are feeding alfalfa or other legume hay, the energy supplied will be about the same, but the protein will be very different. Dobbin will need 14 to 15 pounds daily, which will provide more than enough protein (recall that legume hays contain around 20 percent protein), so I'd recommend reducing the legume hay quantity a bit. Make up the difference with some grass hay, if available. He should get no less than 75 percent forage, so provide a minimum of 15 pounds per day. On this mixed grass/legume diet, Dobbin will undoubtedly gain weight. This is why too much legume hay leads to problems if you are not careful. Some legume hay is fine, but it needs to be calculated and balanced with grass hay.

Dobbin is going to do fine on his hay diet, but you should make sure that fresh water is always available, as well as a free-choice salt and a vitamin/mineral source of some kind. Or provide him with one good vitamin/mineral source in his handful of grain or feed a balancer pellet, as discussed earlier. Check his requirements in the Feed Requirements for Horses table in the Appendix.

When feeding concentrate feeds, unless you have a particular reason for choosing a specific feed, stick to the most commonly sold brand of quality feed available in your area. Brand name feeds are usually a safe bet and are consistent in quality. There isn't much difference among the major brands, so pick one you can readily find. Pellets are preferable to sweet feed because of the high sugar content of sweetfeed, though at 1 pound per day, there isn't enough sugar to be problematic.

In the spring and early summer, there should be sufficient grazing available. Pasture is roughly 25 percent dry matter, and a horse grazing on good pasture will consume roughly 4.4 pounds each hour. Thus Dobbin will consume about 1.1 pounds of dry matter per hour of grazing. Horses spend 60 to 80 percent of their time outside grazing, so in a 24-hour period, Dobbin will graze for 14 to 20 hours. Thus he could easily consume the 14 to 20 pounds of dry matter he requires. That means Dobbin will not require additional hay or grain for nutritional purposes, although it might be a good idea to give him a handful of balancer pellets in a bucket on a daily basis just to bring him to the fence so you can check him over.

Once the grass has gone to seed, the nutritional value will diminish. When you notice the grass beginning to make seeds and becoming stalky and brown, increase Dobbin's grain portion or start feeding him hay. In the fall when the grass greens up again, or if you notice him gaining weight, you can again reduce the hay and grain. But it's probably still a good idea to give Dobbin a handful of pellets every day, so that he is easy to catch and will readily come to the gate.

Dobbin Goes to Work

If Dobbin begins a regular work schedule, you can calculate the extra energy and protein he will need. Let's say he performs one hour a day of light work. Calculate thus: 0.27×10 $(1,000/100 = 10) = 2.7$ Mcal. Therefore, Dobbin will require an extra 0.27 Mcal/100lbs BW/day. His total requirement now is $15 + 2.7 = 17.7$ Mcal.

He will eat 20 pounds of early-cut hay, which provides 20 Mcal; he needs another 1.7 Mcal. One pound of grain will supply 1.7 Mcal. If he is grazing and there is plenty of grass, he can easily consume 20 pounds of DM per day.

In theory, we should deduct the pound of grain from his total intake, leaving a hay intake of 19 pounds. This would mean that he would only receive 19 Mcal from the hay, leaving him short by 1 Mcal, but in truth Dobbin will probably happily eat the full 20 pounds of hay plus the pound of grain. With his one hour of light work per day, he will do fine on 20 pounds of hay and 1 pound of grain, or 20 pounds of grazing and 1 pound of grain. In fact, if you are already giving him one pound of grain to carry his vitamin/mineral supplement, the added one hour a day of work might be just what he needs to keep from gaining weight.

Once Dobbin's ration is arrived at, feeding will then become a matter of constant adjustment. Use his body condition to assess the suitability (or otherwise) of the ration. Remember the saying "The eye of the Master maketh the horse fat!" Check on Dobbin regularly. Learn to use a body score system to assess his condition. There is a comprehensive version in Chapter 5. Or refer to the abbreviated form at the end of the chapter.

Feeding Smokey Joe

Smokey Joe is a mature Thoroughbred gelding, approximately 900 pounds. He is a junior show horse, lives in a stall, and gets two to three hours of turnout per day in a dirt lot. He works moderately for roughly one hour per day; therefore, he requires approximately

Smokey Joe is a mature Thoroughbred gelding, a junior show horse, who lives in a stall and gets two to three hours of turnout per day in a dirt lot.

0.9 Mcal/100lbs BW/day per hour of activity more than the maintenance level.

This means he needs an extra $0.9 \times 9 = 8.1$ Mcal and a total of 21.6 Mcal of DE per day ($0.015 \times 900 = 13.5 + 8.1 = 21.6$ Mcal), which could be provided in 22.0 pounds of early-cut grass hay or 30 pounds of late cut. However, Smokey Joe is only 900 pounds and will probably consume only 18 to 22 pounds of hay per day.

If the hay is early cut and he has a good appetite and eats it well, it will provide 1.0 Mcal/lb. So 22 pounds would provide him with 22 Mcal per day, which is appropriate. If he is also getting one pound of grain per day to carry his vitamin/mineral supplement, then he will be receiving ample energy for his needs.

But if the hay is not early cut, 22 pounds will only provide 15.4 Mcal, leaving a deficit of 6.2 Mcal. Make up for this energy shortfall with three to four pounds of concentrated feed. Remember that we will now need to deduct the pounds of concentrate from the 22 pounds of total daily hay intake: 22 lbs−4 lbs = 18 lbs. The 18 pounds of poor hay will provide 12.6 Mcal ($18 \times 0.7 = 12.6$). So we will need to provide supplemental feed to the value of 9 Mcal ($21.6−12.6 = 9$ Mcal). This means we would need to provide a total of 5.25 pounds of grain to meet Smokey Joe's energy needs. (This is why hay quality is so important.)

Another option is to add some rice bran or oil to the grain to increase the energy density. Fat contains 4.0 Mcal/lb. We could add 4 ounces of fat, which would supply 1.0 Mcal to the grain. Adding 4 ounces of fat means you would only have to give him 4.7 pounds of grain to meet his energy needs.

Is he getting enough protein? His protein requirements are 1.9 pounds ($40 \times 21.6 = 864g = 1.9$ lb) protein. Twenty-two pounds of early-cut hay provides 2.2 pounds of protein, and each pound of 12 percent grain will provide a further 0.12 pounds. This totals 2.3 pounds of protein, which is ample.

If late-cut hay, with 7 percent protein value, is fed, then there is a possibility of a marginal protein deficit, as shown by the following calculation: 18×7 percent $= 1.26$ pounds of protein; the 5.25 pounds of 12 percent grain will supply another 0.63 pounds, which means he gets a total of 1.89 pounds of protein. This is one instance where it might be advisable to add in a few ounces of a protein supplement per day or to change his grain to one with a higher protein content. There is a slight increase in the horse's need for protein with work, and there is some argument for an improvement in protein quality. These needs are best served by feeding a good quality concentrate ration with an ample supply of the essential amino acids or offering an amino acid supplement. (See Chapter 5.) Probably the best way to adjust Smokey Joe's protein level is to use a 14 percent protein concentrate.

Checking for Minerals

Now let's check his mineral status.

Smokey Joe's basic requirements are 20g/day of calcium (Ca), 14g/day of potassium (P), and 10g/day of magnesium (Mg). (Refer to the table in the Appendix for mineral requirements.) We'll assess each mineral separately, beginning with calcium, and assume he is eating 18 pounds of hay and 5.25 pounds of a grain mix.

Most grass hays contain an average of 0.30 percent calcium (legumes have much more), and straight grains (oats or corn) contain on average 0.07 percent. The 18 pounds of grass hay will provide 24.46g (18/100 × 0.3 = 0.054 lbs × 453g = 24.46g). The 5.25 pounds of grain will provide 1.66g (5.25/100 × 0.07 = 0.0037 lbs × 453g = 1.66g).

When you add those up (24.46 + 1.66 = 26.12g of Ca), you'll find that his calcium supply is ample.

For phosphorus, we'll calculate using the feed values and requirements from the tables in the Appendix.

Most grass hays contain 0.22 percent phosphorus. On average, oats and corn grain contain 0.31 percent. His hay will provide 17.9g (18/100 × 0.22 = 0.0396 lbs × 453g = 17.93g). His grain will provide 7.37g (5.25/100 × 0.31 = 0.0163 lbs × 453 = 7.37g). The total in Smokey Joe's ration is 17.9g + 7.37g, for a total 25.27g of phosphorus.

Note that the potassium levels are as high as the calcium. Ideally, his calcium:phosphorus ratio should be 1.1:1. However, on this diet it is very close to 1:1. This is fine for an adult, but could be a problem if Smokey Joe were a young horse. So if you are feeding straight grains to young horses, you will need to add some calcium, probably in the form of ground limestone, to increase the calcium levels. Ground limestone contains 40 percent calcium; to add an extra 2.5g, we need 2.5 × 40 percent = 10. So we need to add 10g of ground limestone per day to Smokey Joe's feed, which is roughly 2 teaspoons, or ½ a tablespoon.

If you are feeding a commercial grain mix, however, it will probably have already been fortified with extra calcium.

Now let's assess magnesium, a mineral that is not commonly checked.

Smokey Joe's requirement is 10g/day. Grass hays contain on average 0.08 percent. Grain usually contains 0.1 percent. So his hay will provide 6.5g (18/100 × 0.08 = 0.0144 lbs × 453g = 6.52g). His grain will provide 2.4g (5.25/100 × 0.1 × 453g = 2.378g).

The total is 8.9g, which would seem to be almost enough. However, magnesium from plant sources is considered to be only 40 percent absorbable, so he will only actually receive 8.9 × .40 = 3.56g, which is not enough. Smokey Joe might well benefit from a magnesium supplement.

The most common supplemental form to use is magnesium oxide, which is 52 percent magnesium and thought to be 60 percent absorbable. To provide the extra 6.44g of magnesium he needs, we need to feed 21.46g of magnesium oxide, or roughly 1 ounce per day (6.44 / 50 percent / 60 percent = 21.46g).

Worth the Effort

As you can see, balancing rations is definitely not for the math-phobic and can take a lot of time. But particularly if you choose to feed whole grains, it is probably worth the effort to make sure your rations are not low in some vital nutrient.

Smokey Joe and Dobbin are relatively easy horses to calculate for. There are many special feeding concerns specific to more needy horses, such as the growing weanling/yearling, the pregnant/lactating mare, the horse in hard competition training, or the severely debilitated horse recovering from illness or starvation. Each of these special needs is best calculated when you have peace and quiet, a set of tables, and a calculator. The best plan, when your horses have special considerations, is to call your local equine nutritionist and get some help.

General Feeding Advice

When feeding Thoroughbred, show, and working horses, provide the upper end of the feeds ranges, rather than the lower, to meet their energy and nutritional requirements best.

This is not the case when feeding most warmbloods and warmblood crosses, however. These horses process feed much more efficiently. To avoid fat horses, therefore, feed a lower quantity of protein and increase the quality and provide more fiber. If possible, select a concentrate with a high fiber inclusion for these guys, such as feeds based on sugar beet pulp or whole oats rather than corn and soybean.

For Quarter Horses, Andalusians, Morgans, Arabs, and all pony breeds (and of course warmbloods), feed from the lower end of the feed range. For these breeds, be sure that there is minimal sugar and ample simple carbohydrates in the diet. Feed high-fiber feeds and make sure that the magnesium levels are sufficient.

Arabians are among the breeds that must be fed from the lower end of the feed range.

THE SIMPLIFIED BODY SCORE METHOD

Apart from measuring or guesstimating the bodyweight, I recommend you use a body score system to assess a horse's condition. You'll find a complete body score assessment version in Chapter 5. Here is a fast and easy version. Try to develop the habit of scoring horses whenever you observe them. With practice it becomes easy. Using a body score system will also be invaluable for better communication when you are consulting a vet or nutritionist. It's a good idea to record the body score number when you do your routine checks.

Ideally, a riding horse should score in the range between 5 and 7. A body score over 8 is a concern, unless the horse is deliberately plumper to prepare for the winter. Any score of 4 or below is cause for worry, especially if winter is around the corner.

To begin, observe the horse's topline. Are the tops of the boney spinal processes level with the back, sunken below, or protruding above?

If the spinal processes are protruding above the level of the back, then score a 4 or below. A significantly protruding spine scores a 3 or lower. If the transverse processes of the vertebrae — the side wings of the vertebrae that should normally be well covered with muscle and fat — are visible, then the horse is emaciated (score a 1 or a 2) and must be treated as a special case.

If the spine is level with the back, score a 5 or 6.

Feel around the top of the tail head. Is the fat there soft or hard? A score of 5 reflects a firm, moderately sized deposit of fat. If the fatty area forms a softer, bigger bulge, score a 6.

If the spine lies just below the back muscles, and you can still feel the ribs, then score a 7. This is a good weight for most working horses to be. If the spine is noticeably lower, there is padding over the ribs, and the tail head is soft, score an 8 and adjust his feed to a lower level to reduce his calorie input a bit.

If there is a trough over the spine that can collect and hold rainwater for three days after it rains, then score a 9 or a 10. Such a horse is seriously overweight and needs to have its diet altered! Grab your calculator and redesign your feed program right away.

Some horses react to high protein and high carbohydrates by becoming spooky or aggressive. If this is happening to a horse in your care, immediately cut out all molasses and corn-based feeds and shift to grass hay only. Slowly reintroduce a high-fiber grain with a suitable vitamin/mineral blend once the undesirable behavior has gone. You might want to refer this problem to a nutritionist. Adding extra magnesium and B vitamins often helps to reduce aggressive or over-exuberant behavior.

If you are feeding such a horse and you want to increase weight gain and avoid the exuberant behavior, then add fat. Additional fat will increase calories without exciting him. The best fats are the least processed options. Remember from Chapter 3 that fat is best fed as naturally as possible. Feed rice bran, whole roast soy, or whole flaxseed rather than processed oils like corn oil from the supermarket. Avoid animal fats in equine diets.

Most show horse owners prefer their horses on the plump side and are very concerned about coat quality and hoof growth. They tend to use lots and lots of supplements! Tailor your supplement choice to the individual horse, choose one or two good quality ones, and stick to them. Try to select products with a high level of polyunsaturated fatty acids, as these have the best effect on coat quality.

Basic Feeding and Management Guidelines

All horses will benefit from the following basic rules for managing health and feeding:

• Deworm on a regular basis; remember to rotate wormers, using a different active chemical at least once per year.
• Treat for bots after the first frost.
• Ensure a regular supply of clean water.
• Feed plenty of long fiber, hay or grass, since this is what horses do best on. At least 50 percent of the diet should be hay/grass.
• Add concentrates (grain or sweet feeds) only as needed.
• Feed only mold-free, clean, good-quality feeds.

• Make sure each horse receives his share. Feeding in a stall is recommended for the bottom horses in the pasture pecking order, unless there is plenty of room to leave many hay piles outside so they can consume enough before other horses claim the hay.

• Feed on a regular timetable. You don't have to be exact but feed roughly (within an hour) the same time each day.

• Keep grain in rodent-proof containers, and keep the grain storage area clean and swept.

• Measure out feeds consistently, preferably by weight.

-5-

Feeding
for a Lifetime

THE NUTRITIONAL NEEDS OF THE HORSE WILL VARY not only with breed and environment, but also with age. From the pregnant mare nourishing a developing fetus, through the growing foal's bone and muscle development, to the high-energy requirements of the horse in hard training, and on through the less efficient food-processing abilities of the older horse, this chapter will explore the nutritional requirements of the various stages of the horse's life.

Throughout this chapter, requirements will be provided on a bodyweight basis, assuming horses are between 800 and 1,350 pounds. They are presented in a table format in the Appendix. If you need more detailed requirement tables, refer to the comprehensive sets of tables for various bodyweights provided in the National Research Council (NRC) publication *Nutrient Requirements of Horses* and in *Feeding and Care of the Horse* by Lon D. Lewis (see Appendix).

Equine Body Score System

The previous chapter offered an abbreviated version of the body score system. This chapter will frequently refer to equine body scores, so here's the comprehensive version. Try to develop the habit of using it to assess the weight and well-being of every horse you know, especially those you care for.

116

❏ SCORE: 1   APPEARANCE: **POOR**

Animal is extremely emaciated: backbone, ribs, the tailhead, point of hips, and point of buttocks project prominently; bone structure of withers, shoulders, and neck are very prominent; no fatty layer can be felt.

❏ SCORE: 2   APPEARANCE: **VERY THIN**

Animal is emaciated; slight fatty layer covers the base of the backbone; the base of the backbone in the lumbar region feels slightly rounded; backbone, ribs, tailhead, point of hips, and buttocks are prominent; withers, shoulders, and neck structures are slightly prominent.

❏ SCORE: 3   APPEARANCE: **THIN**

Fat buildup is apparent about halfway along the backbone; the base of the spine cannot be felt; slight fat covers ribs; ribs are easily discernible; tailhead is prominent but individual vertebrae cannot be observed; point of hips appear rounded but easily discernible; points of buttocks are not apparent; withers, shoulders, and neck are not obviously thin.

❏ SCORE: 4   APPEARANCE: **MODERATELY THIN**

Slight ridge visible along back; faint outline of ribs visible; tailhead prominence depends on conformation, but a fat layer can be felt around it; point of hip is not discernible; withers, shoulders, and neck are not obviously thin.

❏ SCORE: 5   APPEARANCE: **MODERATE**

Back is flat (no crease or ridge); ribs are not visually apparent but are easily felt; fat around tailhead feels slightly spongy; withers appear rounded over top; shoulders and neck blend smoothly into the body.

❏ SCORE: 6   APPEARANCE: **MODERATELY FLESHY**

Horse may have slight crease down the back; fat layer over the ribs is spongy; fat around tailhead feels soft; fat begins to be layered along the side of the withers, behind the shoulders, and along the sides of neck.

❏ SCORE: 7   APPEARANCE: **FLESHY**

Horse may have crease down the back; individual ribs can be felt but there is a noticeable filling of fat between ribs; fat around the tailhead is soft; fat layer apparent along withers, behind shoulders, and along neck.

❏ SCORE: 8   APPEARANCE: **FAT**

Crease visible down the back; ribs can't easily be felt; fat around the tailhead is very soft; area along withers is filled with fat; area behind the shoulders is filled with fat; noticeable thickening of neck; fat layer apparent on inner thighs.

❏ SCORE: 9   APPEARANCE: **EXTREMELY FAT**

Obvious crease visible down the back; patchy fat appears over ribs; bulging fat is noticeable around the tailhead, along the withers, behind the shoulders, and along the neck; fat on inner thighs may rub together; flank filled with fat.

And the Score Is . . .

A body score of less than 4 indicates inadequate energy intake, and a score of more than 7 indicates an excessive energy intake. Adjust feed levels accordingly. A score between 5 and 7 indicates the proper amount of energy intake. Keep up the good work!

Life Stage Requirements

Let's look at the basic needs of horses during their various life stages.

Resting Adult, or Maintenance Feeding

This horse is the classic pasture potato. Being overweight is usually the non-working adult horse's biggest issue. A body score of 5 or 6, perhaps a 7, but certainly no more, is best for non-working horses. Remember Dobbin from Chapter 4? Hay, grass, and just enough grain to bring him to the gate on a regular basis are all this horse needs. Add one good vitamin/mineral source and resting adults will

A resting adult horse needs only hay, grass, and a small amount of grain.

be fine. Of course, if the horse loses weight or can't maintain his weight on pasture/hay, then he will require supplemental grain, but before you pile on the sweet feed, worm him and have his teeth checked.

The idle adult horse requires an energy intake of 1.5 Mcal/100lbs BW/day. This can be provided by 20 pounds of good grass hay (see Chapter 4 for that calculation) or by allowing him to graze for 18 hours on good-quality pasture.

Working Adult

Adult horses in training or working require extra energy and nutrients to fuel their efforts. How much more they need depends a lot on the individual horse, his metabolism, and how hard he is working. The key factors are the speed and the duration of the work. A horse doing a lot of high-speed work requires much more energy than the horse doing slow work. A racehorse galloping at 25 miles per hour (600 to 700 meters per minute) will require much more supplemental energy than a school horse will, even though the

Working horses need more energy. The faster the work, the more they need!

racehorse only works for three-quarters of an hour a day and the school horse for three to four hours. One way to estimate the extra energy needed by working horses is to feed for maintenance based on bodyweight and then add the extra required for the amount of work done.

For a 1,100-pound (500kg) horse, daily maintenance is:
- Energy: 16.4 Mcal/day
- Crude protein: 656g
- Calcium: 20g
- Potassium: 14g
- Magnesium: 7.5–10g
- Copper: 30ppm (mg/kg)
- Zinc: 40ppm
- Selenium: 0.2ppm.

Fitness is not to be confused with fatness; lean, fit horses will suffer less from heat exhaustion and other problems than overweight horses will. Competition horses should score not more than 6 on the body score scale.

Quality hay and sufficient grain to meet his energy needs are what this horse needs. The extra protein requirements for the working horse should be met by higher feed intake. If your hay or grain is low in minerals, adding minerals in a supplement may also be necessary. Most working horses have higher magnesium, potassium, and sodium requirements, especially if they sweat. If they regularly work up a sweat, give them 2 to 3 ounces of electrolyte mix daily. For homemade formulas, see Chapter 2 under minerals.

Here are some other pointers:
• A horse doing mild work (schooling, pleasure riding) needs between ½–1 pound of grain per hour of work done.
• A horse doing moderate work (dressage, ranch work, hunting, showing) needs 2–3 pounds of grain per hour worked.
• A horse doing hard work (foxhunting, racing, polo, eventing) needs 4 pounds or more of extra grain per hour worked.

Good-quality grain is important for horses in work, as well as a good source of minerals, especially electrolytes. Unless you are training racehorses, endurance horses, or advanced eventers, make up most of the energy deficit with readily fermentable complex carbohydratess, such as soy hulls or sugar beet pulp, or add oil or fat rather than extra starch.

Horses that work at speed require simple carbohydrates to ensure that there is adequate muscle glycogen for the fast-twitch fibers but there is a price to be paid for these. For one thing, starches produce higher stomach acidity and increase the chance of ulcers. Also, a high-carbohydrate diet will generate excess energy, making a horse hotter or harder to handle. You may experience behavior problems in this case. The racehorse, eventer, or endurance horse will benefit from high-quality essential fatty acids in the diet to ensure proper membrane health throughout his body. These horses will do best if the fat is supplied from oil seed grains rather than oil. Feed them 4 ounces a day of whole flaxseed (50 percent fat), whole roast soy, or rice bran rather than corn oil.

If you feed diets high in starch, include extra antacids, usually salts of magnesium and calcium, such as calcium carbonate (limestone) and magnesium oxide or sulfate, in the feed, either blended in or as a supplement. There is little risk of overdosing calcium and magnesium because they are very soluble and will be excreted in the urine or lost in the sweat. They can halt the formation of ulcers by neutralizing the stomach acids. By reducing stomach discomfort from excess acid, they reduce the chances of cribbing behavior.

FEEDING FOR FUEL

Current research shows that some recurring management conditions (such as colic, tying-up, founder, and certain misbehaviors) are actually symptoms of an overload of simple carbohydrates. This is usually due to trying to feed too much at once. Remember that the horse has a very small stomach; and if too much is fed in one meal, the excess gets pushed through into the hind-gut. An overload of simple carbs sets the fermentation process into high gear, which can lead to several kinds of gastrointestinal tract problems, like excessive gas, colic, founder, or diarrhea. If the horse needs to consume an excess of 10 pounds of grain per day to fulfill his energy needs, the amount should be split into three or more meals. No single meal should contain over 5 pounds. Adding some easily fermentable fiber (complex carbs) and fat helps the digestion process, reduces the insulin response to the starch, and is a much safer way to supply the energy.

Young, rapidly growing grass has a very high sugar content, and a grazing horse can consume quite a quantity during 12 or more hours of grazing. This is why many horses display problems of insulin resistance or a tendency to founder when turned on lush spring pastures. Limit grazing with a muzzle, or create a small dirt lot so horses can self-exercise without access to the lusher pastures. It can be a mistake to improve horse pastures too much. Weedy, dry grass may not look as pretty, but is often safer, especially for ponies and heavier types of horses, due to their sensitivity to sugar.

Of particular concern are draft horses or other horses that show a tendency to tie-up or to have stiff, sore muscles after even moderate workloads. These horses may have a genetic tendency to malformation of glycogen and will do better if fed only complex carbs, adequate protein, fats, minerals, and a minimum of simple carbs.

Horses that work slowly or only occasionally do not do as well on high-carbohydrate diets. Horses of draft, warmblood, or pony breeding will be particularly sensitive to excess simple carbohydrates. These horses need to receive the bulk of their diet as fiber, with supplementary fat added to address any energy deficits.

Horses on high-fat diets will need to have their minerals carefully balanced, and their protein source needs to be of slightly higher quality in order to help them to perform at their best. If you want to add fat to these horses' diet, it is better to add some whole flaxseed, whole roast soy, or rice bran rather than cups of processed oils such as those sold in supermarkets. Remember from Chapter 2 that processed fats lose much of their nutritive value because they are chemically treated to extend shelf life. They are best avoided.

The Pregnant Mare: First Nine Months

The pregnant mare must consume adequate nutrition both to maintain her own bodyweight and to provide the necessary nutrients for the growing fetus. In horses, the majority of the fetal growth takes place in the last three to four months of the

If she is healthy and well nourished, a pregnant mare will be able to provide adequate nutrition for herself and her foal-to-be.

pregnancy. From conception until then, the fetus grows very slowly, with a dramatic growth spurt about four months before birth. So caretakers need not worry too much about extra feed for the mare during the first seven months of gestation.

As long as the mare is in good condition herself and receives adequate energy, minerals, and vitamins, she will be able to provide appropriate nutrition to her fetus just fine. Feed her as if she is on maintenance, but pay special attention to the mineral balance and particular attention to the quality of the feed. This is certainly the worst possible time to introduce toxins from moldy feed, hay, or other sources.

A pregnant mare should merit a body score of around 6 on the scale, and she may increase to a 7 with no deleterious effects. So use the body score scale to help you adjust her feed intake as necessary.

For the first nine months of pregnancy, the mare will require 1.65 Mcal/100lbs BW for energy and around 8 percent protein. The hay to grain ratio should be a minimum of 50:50, but feeding better-quality hay can help reduce the grain requirement. Remember, fiber is a mom-to-be's best diet.

For an 1,100 pound (500kg) mare, the energy she needs equals 18.2 Mcal DE/day, and 810g (1.79lbs) of crude protein. Calcium intake should be 36g/day, potassium 26g/day, magnesium 9g/day, copper 30 ppm (mg/kg), zinc 40 ppm, and selenium 0.2 ppm.

Final Trimester

During the final three months, the mare will need 1.8 Mcal/100 lbs BW of energy intake and between 10 and 11 percent good-quality protein. Start increasing the quality (not necessarily the quantity) of the feed from about month nine onwards; as with all horses, introduce the new feed gradually. Introduce a higher-quality hay, or switch from a basic grain ration to one especially designed for pregnant mares. At the very least, start giving her a vitamin/mineral supplement designed for pregnant mares.

During the last four months, pay particular attention to the mineral content and balance of the mare's feed. Offering a chelated mineral source is well worth the extra expense at this point in her pregnancy.

During the last trimester a 1,100-pound (500kg) mare will need:
- Energy: 19.7 Mcal/day
- Crude protein: 866g (1.9 lbs)
- Calcium: 37g/day
- Potassium: 28g/day
- Magnesium: 9.5g/day
- Copper, zinc, and selenium levels remain the same as the beginning

During the last trimester, take the mare off fescue if she is on it, and feed a good-quality supplement designed for pregnant mares. Maintain the mare at 6 or 7 on the body score scale, which might mean steadily escalating the feed value from month seven until birth (parturition). If she is an easy keeper, you might not need to increase the amount of feed much, but make sure she gets her minerals and vitamins. Studies have shown that mares in the last trimester of pregnancy that maintain a body score of 6 to 7 experience fewer problems with parturition and lactation.

Once the mare has successfully foaled, she then becomes a lactating mare.

The Lactating Mare

Because the lactating mare has the highest nutritional demands of all horses, this is when she needs the most help to receive adequate supplies. She should be given a very high-quality feed source with a correctly balanced mineral supply (most feeds are too low in copper, zinc, and magnesium and high in sodium, potassium, and calcium). She needs a readily digestible energy source, preferably *not* based on simple carbohydrates; this translates to a diet high in easily digestible fiber, with some added fat, preferably from oil seed grains or rice bran.

During the first three months of lactation she will require 2.6 Mcal/100 lbs BW for energy and around 13 percent protein. For an 1,100-pound (500Kg) mare, this translates to:
- Energy: 28.6 Mcal/day
- Crude protein: 1,427g (3.15 lbs)
- Calcium: 56g/day

- Potassium: 36g/day
- Magnesium: 11g/day
- Copper: 30 ppm
- Zinc: 60 ppm
- Selenium: 0.2 ppm

Attention to protein quality really matters at this time. Feed her the better (usually translated as more expensive) protein sources to ensure a supply of good-quality milk for the foal. She needs a balanced supply of readily absorbable minerals; this is where the use of chelated mineral sources will really pay off. So pay close attention to the quality of the feed; the foal will receive a lot of what the mare eats through the milk, and if she is ingesting toxins the foal will receive them too.

The mare's supply of milk drops after the first three months of lactation, so introducing the foal to a little grain or allowing him to eat with his dam will help him to augment the milk as it dwindles and prepare him to be able to eat properly at weaning. The foal

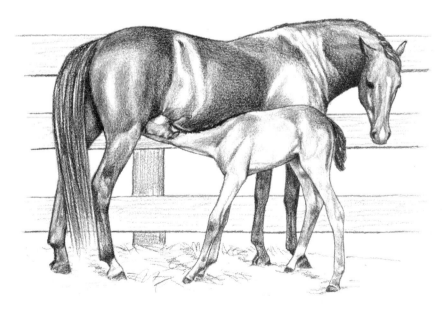

A lactating mare has the highest nutritional needs of all horses.

should not need a separate feeder unless the mare is really greedy and won't share; keep a close eye on them at feeding time to see how much the foal actually receives.

During the last three months of lactation, the mare will require 2.2 Mcal/100 lbs BW energy and 11 percent protein. For an 1,100-pound (500Kg) mare this means:

- Energy: 24.2 Mcal/day
- Crude protein: 1.050g (2.32 lbs)
- Calcium: 36g/day
- Potassium: 22g/day
- Magnesium: 9.5g/day

Ideally, a mare should be at a body score of 7 at parturition and not drop below a 5 during lactation. Pay close attention to her during this period. Milk production takes quite a lot of energy from her, and if she is inadequately supplied she will lose condition as she produces the milk. Mares in the 6 to 7 range will have fewer problems conceiving again, compared to mares who drop to a body score of 4 or below.

The Weanling

Most weanlings are typically overfed rather than underfed! Weanlings need good-quality feed providing up to 3.7–3.8 Mcal/100 lbs BW for energy, and a chelated mineral source. They need about 14.5 percent high-quality protein from a good source that also offers a beneficial array of essential amino acids.

For a weanling of 385 pounds (175kg) destined for a mature weight of 1,100 pounds (500kg), this means:

- Energy: 14.4 Mcal/day
- Crude protein: 730g (1.6 lbs)
- Calcium: 32g/day
- Potassium: 17g/day
- Magnesium: 4.0g/day
- Copper: 50 ppm
- Zinc: 60 ppm

Maintain a correct copper/zinc ratio: that is, slightly more zinc than copper. Note that as the weanling grows, his bodyweight will increase and you will need to adjust his feed accordingly. Keep a weight tape handy and measure him on a monthly basis; adjust the feed according to a) his body score and b) his bodyweight. If the body score indicates he is getting too fat, then cut the feed even if his bodyweight is going up! The body score is the more important indicator. Overfed weanlings become unsound older horses. Weanlings should score *no higher* than 5 to 6 on the body score scale. The excessively padded, stressed weanling you may see in halter classes or the sale ring is not the standard you want for your little guy, since those horses are predisposed to various unsoundnesses and problems like founder or metabolic bone disease (see Chapter 8).

Keep weanlings a little lean, but be certain that they are healthy and look strong, with shiny coats. Make sure they have ample, safe exercise, preferably in a paddock with other horses that won't harass or bully them.

The weanling should grow slowly and steadily, but stay on the lean side.

Grass hay is best for this age. Up to 20 percent of the hay provided can be legume hay. Keep in mind that alfalfa contains a lot of inessential amino acids, which will be excreted. A little alfalfa is fine, though.

Through his first winter, the weanling needs to be fed a very good-quality, well-balanced feed. Attention to the quality of the protein source will pay off for the rest of his life. Along with the high-quality protein, provide a well-balanced, quality mineral source and ample vitamins. Addition of some extra fat or oil, preferably as an oil seed or rice bran instead of corn oil, will help the youngster to grow well and develop the healthy, shiny coat he should have.

Depending on genetics (breeding), weanlings will grow fast or slow. Slow is better! Horses need to grow slowly and steadily, since too high an intake of simple carbohydrates like starch and sugar will produce fat babies, which is not healthy. Use your body score scale to help you decide if the baby is fat enough or too fat.

Your baby should be between 5 and 6 on the scale. Adjust his feed to keep him at that score. Good-quality complex carbohydrates are best, as in good grass hay and a concentrate ration based on sugar beet pulp or other fiber sources, with extra attention to protein quality and to the balance and amount of the minerals.

The Young Horse: Yearling to Two-Year-Old

Nutritionally speaking, there is not much difference between a yearling and a two-year-old. A yearling requires around 12.5 percent good-quality protein and an energy intake of 2.25–2.7 Mcal/100 lbs BW/day, depending on the expected mature size. A two-year-old requires around 12 percent protein and 1.9–2.7 Mcal/100 lbs BW/day, depending on expected mature size, as well as whether or not the two-year-old is in training. (For more details, see Table 4 in the Appendix.) For a yearling of approximately 700 pounds (300kg) expected to grow to 1,100 pounds (500kg) mature weight, this means:
- Energy: 19 Mcal/day
- Crude protein: 900g (2.0lbs)
- Calcium: 32g/day

- Potassium: 18g/day
- Magnesium: 6.0g/day
- Selenium: 0.2 ppm
- Copper: 30 ppm
- Zinc: 40 ppm

Overweight yearlings and two-year-olds often develop into unsound adults or experience problems when they go into training. Keep them lean! A body score of 5 to 6 is ample; if they reach 7, cut down the grain. They require a small amount of good-quality feed, with ample minerals. Avoid excessive protein, and be sure it offers a beneficial amount of essential amino acids.

The diet should not contain too many simple carbohydrates like sugar and starch. Instead, carbohydrates in the diet should be complex, like fiber. So avoid overfeeding corn or molasses.

The yearling should be kept lean.

Provide feeds based on oats or sugar beet pulp instead. Plenty of good hay is important.

By this stage of life, the bulk of skeletal growth has already occurred and subsequent growth is slow. This is not a stage to have the baby overweight. There is considerable muscle to add on to the maturing body in the next years, but the bulk of the bony skeleton is now complete and ready to harden up and layer calcium and magnesium into the bones.

The growth plates in the horse's long bones begin to close from 24 months on. Once they are closed, the young horse can begin a limited amount of work, but he should not start work *until* they are closed. The best way is to radiograph (x-ray) the knees to see if they have closed, or you can feel the knees and see if they are still "open." Obviously x-rays provide the more accurate diagnosis.

If you plan to work your two-year-old, you will need to monitor the growth plates carefully and tailor the workload accordingly. Some breeds don't achieve closure of the growth plates until three, four, or more years of age. These horses should not be worked or ridden as two-year-olds, because again this will lead to unsoundness later in life.

The bones and tendons harden and mature under gentle stress, however, so exercise is very important. Young horses grow best if they receive ample turnout, preferably in company, ideally with other compatible youngsters, plus an older horse to serve as "herd uncle." The older horse will teach them manners and social behavior. Youngsters raised at pasture in the company of other horses have far fewer socialization problems later on.

Between Two and Four

At this stage of life, there is not much difference between feeding the young growing horse and the resting adult. Energy intake should be around 1.5–1.9 Mcal/100 lbs BW/day with protein content around 8 to 11 percent.

The two-to-four-year-old's energy requirements are similar to an adult's.

For a youngster of 990 pounds (425kg) with an estimated mature weight of 1,100 pounds (500kg), on a daily basis this means:
- Energy: 15.0 Mcal/day
- Crude protein: 900g (2.1 lbs)
- Calcium: 26g/day
- Potassium 15g/day
- Magnesium 8.0g/day
- Selenium: 0.2 ppm
- Copper: 30 ppm
- Zinc: 40 ppm

Pay a little more attention to the mineral balance, and, most of all, don't let youngsters get too fat. Stick to the body score of between 5 and 6. Adequate simple carbohydrates, lots of fiber, a balanced, digestible mineral source, and lots of exercise in the company of their peers are the best way to feed and raise young horses.

If the horse is in training, then he requires a higher level of energy intake. The higher protein requirement is usually met by an increased feed intake, but pay attention to the quality of the protein; use of an essential amino acid supplement will assist in the proper development of muscle and ensure good hoof growth.

The main thing with two-to-four-year-olds is to make sure that they stay lean and don't become overweight.

The Senior Horse

As the horse ages, his ability to digest and chew may become compromised. The senior horse, which these days means a horse older than 20 years, needs feeds based on more readily digestible grains and softer, more digestible hays. Older horses often need feeds containing additives that help them digest food more easily, such as yeasts and probiotics. If they are Cushinoid (see Chapter 8), they will require a low glycemic diet with extra fatty acids and better-quality protein. A chelated mineral source will help the aging GI tract to absorb the minerals the animal needs. If their teeth are so worn down that aged horses have trouble chewing, then the feeds will need to be very soft. It helps if they are fed wet or soaked. The modern process of extruding feed will help these horses.

As most senior horses are Cushinoid or nearly so, the use of feeds based on sugar beet pulp or soy hulls is preferable to feed based on corn. When grains are fed, it is best if they are cooked so they can be more easily digested. Choices like cooked or flaked barley or corn are more digestible than ground or cracked grains.

Because the senior horse may have deteriorating kidneys, it is best to feed a small amount of high-quality protein that can be completely used by the body rather than a lot of low-grade protein that the kidneys have to process. Use of the better-quality vitamin sources and chelated minerals will also help the aging GI tract.

Emphasize dental care to ensure that what teeth are left can chew and grind as well as possible. Years of neglect to their mouths often leave old horses with such poor dentition that their ability to eat is compromised. Find a really good vet trained in dental work for these guys. Wet the hay and feed chopped hay products so the older horse can ingest fiber even if it cannot chew it sufficiently.

The energy requirement is very similar to the maintenance level, usually around 1.5 Mcal/100 lbs BW/day. Remember, you can add necessary calories in the form of flax, whole roast soy, black sunflower seeds, or rice bran. Protein requirements in an older horse are still around 10 percent but it will pay off to supply that as a better-quality protein that produces less ammonia and urine.

The older horse needs softer, more digestible feeds.

-6-

Feed Storage
and Feeding Tips

THE MANNER IN WHICH YOU STORE YOUR HORSE'S FEED will make an enormous difference in the value and viability of the grain or forage. In addition to the obvious health benefits, you will save money if you can avoid having to dispose of spoiled feed. Here are some general guidelines on feeding and storage.

Storing Grain

Since grain is easy to buy and transport, it is usually recommended that smaller farms buy about a week's supply at a time. This will ensure freshness, minimize the space needed for storage, and reduce the chances of attracting rodents to the grain storage area. Store grain in a cool, dry, well-ventilated area, because grain will keep its nutritional value best if it does not get overheated, and it must remain dry.

Grain should be stored in rodent-proof, waterproof bins, preferably with secure lids. Old, moldy grain is a substantial health hazard. (See Chapter 8 for more on feed toxins.) Be sure you clean the bins out thoroughly at regular intervals. To prevent mold and rodent infestation, spilled grain should not be allowed to remain in corners or edges for very long, especially when the weather is wet or warm.

Lidded trash cans or barrels make very good grain bins. A 32-gallon bin holds between 50 and 100 pounds of grain. Consider using the plastic versions sold in discount stores; they are very inexpensive and can be scrubbed out at appropriate intervals. If you need to store and feed a range of different

Grain should be stored in rodent-proof, waterproof bins, preferably with secure lids.

feeds, you can designate one trash can for each feed type. Label the cans accordingly, and keep them neatly against the wall. Keep the lids secure to prevent horses from unauthorized access and to keep flies and rodents out.

Keep the area around the bins swept up and free of spilled grain; remember that grain lying around will be very attractive to all kinds of critters and result in a parade of unwanted visitors. The best rodent control you can implement is vigilant cleanliness.

Bigger farms or stables may choose to use larger, custom-built bins. The same rules apply.

Storing Hay

Hay storage requires a large-volume, well-ventilated, roofed space that keeps the rain off. Hay must be stored up off the ground, on a solid floor, on pallets, or on planks. If the hay comes in contact with the bare ground, the bottom bales will be ruined for feeding purposes by wet and mold. Remove old bales every year. If moldy bales remain long enough (a few years), mold can migrate up the bales into the next layer and further.

It is highly recommended that hay be stored at a distance from the horses, and preferably *not* in overhead areas if horses are housed below. The dust and seeds that inevitably drift down from the hay are very bad for horses' lungs and eyes. If you must store hay above the stabling area, be sure the storage floor is solid and sealed.

Another reason to store hay well away from horse stabling areas is that hay can pose a considerable fire hazard. If new hay is stacked in the barn or shed before it is fully dry, it can heat up and spontaneously combust. Minimize fire risks by storing hay away from where horses live.

Since the cheapest way to buy hay is straight off the field at hay-making time, an appropriate, safe hay storage area is a must if you plan to take advantage of this price break. It is often well worth the investment to build or otherwise obtain a suitable, free-standing hay shed or barn, and locate it near — but not *too* near — the horse barn. The hay shed should provide appropriate doorways to allow a truck and trailer or perhaps tractor and trailer to deliver the hay and to allow easy access for whatever vehicle — tractor or wheelbarrow — hauls the day's hay requirements to the horse barn.

If you build your hay shed in the pasture, then fence it off securely to keep hungry, curious horses out. Remember to provide a solid 12- or 14-foot gate for access. Also be sure to plan for enough room within the fenced-off area to allow the delivery truck to maneuver. Remember that the flooring must be suitable to keep the hay dry and up off the ground or you will lose the bottom layer of bales to dampness and rot.

This free-standing hay shed provides easy access for any type of vehicle.

Feeding Grain and Hay

Feeds should always be measured out by weight, not
volume. All nutritionists and
feed companies calculate nutrition information based on
bodyweight and provide recommended feeding amounts
in terms of weight.

Measuring Out Grains

Horsefolk, however, tend to
talk and think in scoops of feed
(volume), rather than weight.
Keep in mind that scoops
come in a variety of sizes (volumes) and that the various
feeds have different densities
(weights). So if you use the

*Hay storage requires a large-volume,
well-ventilated, roofed space that
keeps the rain off. Hay must be
stored up off the ground, on a solid
floor, on pallets, or on planks.*

same size scoop to measure different types of feed, you will actually
scoop and feed varying amounts of each type of feed.

The solution? Weigh all feed! If you don't have a scale in your
feed room, here's another method. Get a simple kitchen scale from
a discount store and install it in your feed room. Then weigh the
empty scoop so you can then deduct the weight of the scoop from
the final figure and know the actual weight of the feed.

Fill the scoop half full and weigh the contents. Subtract the
weight of the scoop and write down the number you end up with,
the weight of a half-scoop. Next, fill it completely so you know
what a full scoop weighs. Make note of your findings and repeat
this process for each amount and feed you use, as they will all be
different.

I recommend that you mark the scoop at the one pound or the
half-pound point (or whatever increments are most useful to you)
so you can be consistent when you (or others) measure.

If you use a different scoop for the oats versus the sweet feed, then also write on the scoop what feed it is used for, as well as marking the levels for various weights of feed to minimize the chance of a mistake being made.

The Appendix offers a table (Table 1) for comparing weights and volumes of different feeds.

Measuring Hay

Hay can be weighed using a hay net and a hanging hook scale. You can get a hanging scale from a good feed or agricultural store. It is always a good idea to weigh a few bales when the hay comes in so you can get an idea of how much the average bale weighs. Be aware that some farmers

Measure feeds by weight, not by volume.

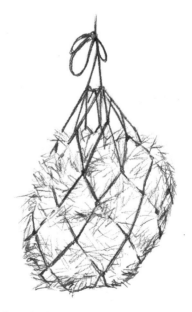

You can weigh hay with a hanging hook scale (left) and a hay net (right).

make their bales tighter and heavier than others. When hay is sold by the bale rather than by weight, buying lightweight bales might prove to be a false economy. Even if they are cheaper, they won't contain as much hay. A bale that is heavy but misshapen or small is probably not a tight bale but a wet bale; this applies particularly if the strings appear loose but the bale is still heavy. Set that bale aside and open it before the others to check whether it is suitable to feed to your horse.

A bale that is heavy but misshapen or small is probably not a tight bale but a wet bale, especially if the strings appear loose but the bale is still heavy.

Feeding Tips

Grain is best fed in round tubs, buckets, or mangers that have no sharp corners that collect uneaten feed. Be sure all feeders have no sharp edges that the horse can injure himself on. Grain feeders should be large enough to allow the horse to easily put his nose deeply into it to reach the bottom and clean up around any edges. Avoid a small bucket, which is likely to get caught on the head or halter, leading to panic and injury. A feeder that is too small can also get damaged from the frustrated horse banging at it to get at the feed inside.

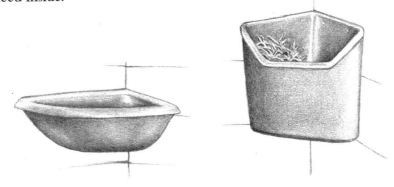

Offer grain in round tubs, buckets, or mangers that have no sharp corners that collect uneaten feed.

The bucket, tub, or manger can be fixed to the wall of the stall or placed on the ground, if the horse won't tip it over while eating. Feeding on or close to the ground is best for the horse, but the closer to the ground, the easier it is for the horse to tip the container over. Hanging the container makes it less likely that the horse will tip it over, stand in it, or get caught in it. Ideally, mangers should be removable so that they can be taken down and cleaned out when necessary, but most are fixed in place. Even if you can't remove the feeder, it should be cleaned out on a regular basis. The triangular corner feeders especially tend to accumulate old feed in the corners. Be aware that not only can old grain rot and smell terrible, putting the horse off his feed, but moldy grain poses a health hazard. (See Chapter 8.)

When feeding grain to horses that are loose in the pasture, it is best to use heavy, round rubber tubs or properly situated troughs or mangers. Buckets hung from the fence are quick, easy, and convenient, but wreck havoc with the fencing, look scruffy, and rapidly deteriorate if left out. If you do use buckets, bring them back in when they're empty.

When feeding a group of hungry horses out in the pasture, make sure that there is ample room for all animals to reach the grain. Otherwise the ones at the bottom of the social ladder won't get enough. If necessary, offer more than one feed trough so there is ample access.

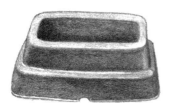

Use heavy, round tubs to feed pastured horses. A hay rack is not ideal because the hay is too high.

Feeding Hay

Hay is best fed on a level lower than the horses' normal head height or lower than the withers of the smallest horse. Hay racks placed higher than that can create problems when the dust and seeds fall into the horses' eyes as they pull out the strands of hay. If no hay trough is available, then feed the hay on the ground. Some may be wasted, but it is healthier for horses to eat with their heads down. When horses eat with their heads down, the unwanted bits can fall out of their mouths and are less likely to end up in the eyes. Be careful to avoid putting hay on sandy ground, though. When horses vacuum the little leftover morsels of hay, they also ingest sand, which can irritate the GI tract and lead to colic.

When group feeding hay out in the field, spread the hay out into several piles, allowing one more pile than there are horses, to

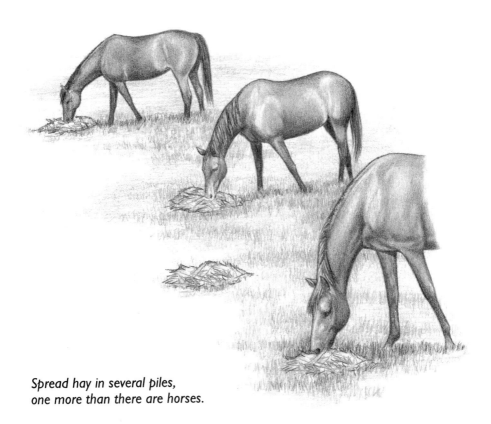

Spread hay in several piles,
one more than there are horses.

ensure that the lowest horse in the herd pecking order can get his or her share. Separate the piles widely enough so that no horse can guard two piles at once. Horses can get very aggressive with each other at feeding times.

Round Bale Basics

If you are feeding round bales, make sure that all horses have adequate access in order to get their share. With a herd of more than five animals, your best bet may be to put out more than one round bale at a time. Be aware that round bales are sub-

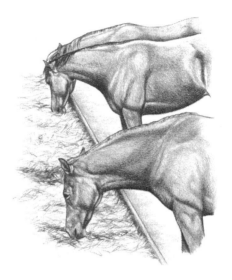

Hay is best fed on a level lower than the horses' normal head height or lower than the withers of the smallest horse.

ject to a quantity of wasted hay and large hay clumps. To minimize these problems, it is best to use a suitable round bale feeder, which keeps the hay dry and up off the ground. If the round bale is uncovered, it needs to be eaten within 5 to 10 days to keep the hay from getting too wet and moldy to be edible without causing possible health problems.

Check the round bale feeders daily to spot bits of baling string that may be wound around them or caught up in them. Of course you will have removed all the visible string when you set the bale up, but pieces can be caught up in the bale at baling time and won't appear until some has been eaten. Use a pitchfork and a wheelbarrow to remove any moldy or wet sections.

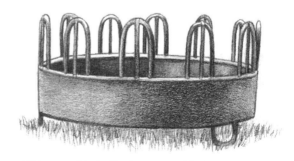

This round-bale feeder is suitable for horses.

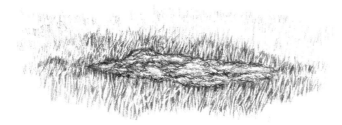

*Round bales can result in wasted hay
and large, unsightly hay clumps.*

Removing a round bale once the string is removed is very hard work. If you must deal with a bad round bale, your best bet might be to borrow some steers to eat it. Otherwise it will mean intense labor with a pitchfork and wheelbarrow.

Soaking Hay

Some horses may need their hay soaked prior to feeding (see Chapter 8 on COPD). If you care for such a horse, soak the hay in a tub or (clean) manure bucket. Put enough hay into the tub for one meal, fill it with water, make sure *all* the hay gets good and wet, let it soak for 10 to 20 minutes, drain off the water, and feed the hay right out of the tub. You can also place the hay in a hay net, soak as above, pull the hay net out of the water (it will be heavy, so be careful). Hang the net up for a minute to drain before hanging it up in the horse's stall. Be sure to mount a very stout hanger from a solid beam or wall. A net of wet hay can be heavy and will pull most screw rings right out of the wall or even pull sections of inadequately secured wall down.

Be sure to hang the net high enough that the bottom does not drag to the ground and pose a

Soak hay for 10 to 20 minutes, drain the water, and feed right out of the tub.

hazard for the horse when it is empty. The hazard that comes from low-hanging nets is why many caretakers prefer to feed even wet hay loose in a tub or on the ground. Remove the net when the horse is finished to avoid any possibility of an entanglement. Wet hay can also be put on a tarp or rubber mat that's placed in a corner.

Feeding Checklist

For many of us, our busy lifestyle may mean that the best time to observe our horses is when we feed them. This is a very good opportunity to check the horse and its surroundings for clues to any potential or actual problems. When you feed your horses, form the habit of running through a mental checklist; this way, you won't miss important signs.

- ❏ Have the horses finished the last meal; is there feed left in the manger?
- ❏ Are there any half-chewed lumps of feed in the manger (a sign of potential dental problems; call the vet/dentist)?
- ❏ Are the horses drinking adequate amounts? Check the water level.
- ❏ Do the horses have a good appetite? Do they wait eagerly for their feed?
- ❏ Do they look normal and healthy overall?
- ❏ Are manure balls normal: firm and round, not in soft piles like cow manure?
- ❏ Is the hay all eaten?
- ❏ In a group feeding situation, does each horse consume his or her fair share of feed?

Based on your findings, carry on with your appropriate feeding program or adjust accordingly.

-7-

Pasture Management

WITHOUT A DOUBT, HORSES THRIVE BEST in a living situation where they have regular access to nutritious pasture in the company of other horses. If they can run and buck and play, bask in the sun, stand in the shade, and graze in the company of other equines, free from predators, illness, and injury, from the horse's point of view,

Horses thrive when they have regular access to safe pasture in the company of other horses.

that is undoubtedly the ideal life. The mental value of turnout in a pasture, especially in company, must not be underestimated.

There is no doubt, however, that pasturing horses is risky. There are so many ways for a horse to injure himself out in a pasture. The benefit to a horse's mental state must be balanced against the risk of injury. For most pleasure horses, the pasture is essential, but for some competition horses, it might not be worth the risk. Even in the best-maintained and fenced pasture, a fit and active horse can injure himself. This is the reason most people with high-powered competition horses are reluctant to turn them out. The decision to avoid turning the horse out, however, does put the horse at risk of a number of behavior problems and some management problems. For example, a study done in England in 2002 showed that foals who were pastured with buddies at weaning were half as likely to develop the habits of cribbing or wood chewing. And other studies have shown that horses at pasture are less likely to colic or suffer from tying up. So keeping your horse in to prevent the risk of injury may expose him to greater risk of other problems.

How much of their nutrition the pasture will supply is highly variable. It will depend on the number of horses per acre, the climate, the soil type, and the time of year. But if properly managed, even a small pasture can supply a lot of the horse's nutritional needs. Pasture also supplies a place for exercise and, if the horse is turned out in a group, companionship. It allows the horse to be a horse, to indulge in social behaviors, and to relax.

Identifying Good Pasture

Above all other concerns, horses require safe pastures, free from hazards that might cause injury, like holes in the ground or tools or farming implements, with secure fencing that they can readily see. Horses are infamously capable of injuring themselves, and safety while grazing is more important than food value. They also require a reliable supply of fresh water (preferably *not* from a pond, for the reasons discussed in Chapter 2), some kind of shelter from sun and wind, and a solid, safe gateway that is easy to pass through.

In the pasture itself, look for green, even growth, free from poisonous weeds. Mature trees can supply welcome shade, but may be dangerous during thunderstorms, as horses tend to shelter under them. If the trees are tall, they are more likely to attract lightning. It is a toss-up to know whether horses are safer in the pasture or in a barn during thunderstorms; if lightning hits the barn, it is just as likely to kill them as if it hits a tree they are sheltering under.

Grazing and Nutrition

Grass begins its growth cycle in the spring; at that time, young grass is bright green. It darkens as it matures and becomes grayish at seeding, before turning to yellow-brown. The yellow-brown indicates that it has little or no feed value left, but while it is green, it is nutritious.

A horse will graze for 60 to 80 percent of the time it spends in the pasture. In a 24-hour period, it will graze for 14 to 19 hours. If on good pasture, the horse will consume up to 4 pounds of grass in an hour of grazing. Since fresh grass is roughly 25 percent dry matter, a grazing horse on good pasture will consume between 1 and 1.3 pounds of dry matter per hour of grazing. Therefore, in a 24-hour period on grass, the horse can consume 15 to 25 pounds of dry matter per day.

For an idle, mature horse, this is sufficient fiber intake to meet most, if not all, of his energy needs. Fresh grass is abundant in protein and vitamins, but can be low in minerals, so as long as trace mineralized salt is available along with fresh water, a horse on good pasture can meet his nutritional needs.

If pasture time is reduced, or if there is insufficient pasture, then grazing may not meet nutritional needs. However, even if you have a limited grazing acreage, there are management strategies that can maximize the nutrition the horse can obtain from it.

Divide your pasture into smaller sections with suitable fencing. This will allow you to rotate grazing areas so the horses can access fresh pasture from time to time. This also allows pastures to rest occasionally and gives the grass a chance to recover. If you can't rotate or make smaller pastures, designate a small, restricted area where you can put the horses and feed them hay during periods when the pasture is stressed. This strategy allows the larger part of the pasture to rest a while.

POISONOUS PLANTS

Poisonous breeds of plants vary throughout the country. To learn which plants are endemic to your area, contact your state extension office for information on the toxic plants that grow in your state. Learn to identify them. There is an excellent chapter on poisonous plants with full color photographs in Lon D. Lewis's *Clinical Equine Nutrition* (see the Appendix).

As a general rule, poisonous plants are broad-leaved plants that are hardy under stressful conditions, such as drought and over-grazing. Horses don't usually browse toxic plants unless they have nothing else to eat, so the best way to keep them from consuming toxic plants is

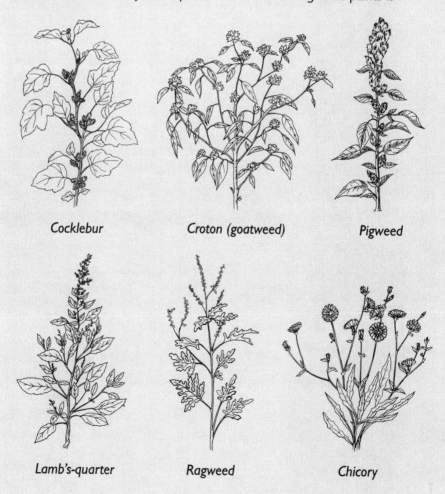

Cocklebur   *Croton (goatweed)*   *Pigweed*

Lamb's-quarter   *Ragweed*   *Chicory*

to make sure that they have plenty of nutritious grass or hay to eat instead. Keep the pastures well mowed, as mowing minimizes the growth and spread of broad-leaved plants.

If you have a heavy infestation of broad-leaved weeds, you may need to dig weeds out or treat the pastures to remove them. One way is to treat with a suitable broad-leaved weed killer or herbicide, followed by an application of fertilizer. This will knock back the weeds and allow the grasses to become reestablished. If you do use herbicides, you will need to remove the animals from the pasture for a period of a few weeks to prevent them from ingesting any herbicide and/or fertilizer and to allow the grasses to recover.

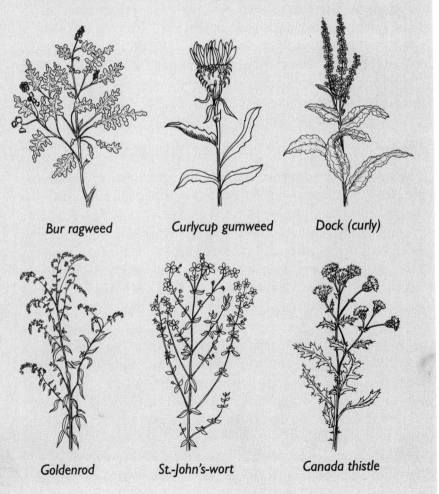

Bur ragweed   Curlycup gumweed   Dock (curly)

Goldenrod   St.-John's-wort   Canada thistle

Turnout for Exercise and Grazing

For most modern horses, especially in urban areas, turnout is primarily for exercise, and the nutritional input of grazing is not as significant. If the pasture is small and used by a lot of horses, you need to provide grasses that can stand up to high traffic, even though these are often not the most nutritious grasses. But pastures are much more useful — and prettier to look at — if they are green and fertile rather than broken up by large bare patches, so maintenance is needed.

For over-grazed turnouts or smaller, urban areas, the kind of maintenance necessary to keep pastures green will focus primarily on appearance and maintaining consistent vegetative cover, even if it isn't the highest-quality grass. However, if you live in a very dry climate, it's likely your turnout area will rapidly become a dry lot, offering little or no vegetation. Rotating grazing areas might prolong vegetative life in that case.

Greener Pastures

Turnout that must support many horses or is stressed by climate extremes is best maintained by erecting suitable fencing to divide it into small lots that can be periodically rested and rotated. Horses are notoriously highly selective grazers. They will select the best grasses, and over time tend to graze all the delicious grasses to death, which allows the weeds and less tasty grasses to take over. Periodic rest periods for grazing areas, along with regular mowing and occasional fertilizing, minimize long-term impact on pasture.

Horses on pasture tend to designate specific toilet areas where they drop manure. They naturally avoid grazing on toilet areas, a habit that reduces the parasite reinfestation rate somewhat, but not completely, as the worm larvae will travel quite a way to find a nice plant to climb up so that they will be eaten. Harrowing pastures will spread the manure and allow it to dry out, which reduces the number of worm eggs.

Ideally, however, you should collect the manure, compost it, and then spread the compost over the land. This returns the valuable nutrients to the soil and kills the worm eggs in the manure.

Buttercups and docks in this pasture indicate acid soil, poor drainage, and over-grazing.

Although parasite eggs are usually well encysted and can survive drying, they can't survive heat, which is why composting eliminates them.

It also minimizes worm infestation when horses can graze along with other species, such as sheep, goats, or cattle. Equine worms will not infect them, and they will kill the eggs they eat.

To maintain a grazing pasture for horses, you need to focus primarily on mowing and harrowing. Regular mowing will help control the tall weeds, and regular harrowing will scatter the manure and allow for more even grass growth.

Fertilizing is less important and may be harmful. Horses are more sensitive to the high sugars in some grasses than cattle are, and it often does not pay to over-improve the grazing in terms of nutrition. Over-dressing with high-nitrogen fertilizers is often more damaging than helpful. Limit your fertilizing program to adding lime and occasionally a mixed fertilizer containing potash and potassium, rather than high levels of nitrogen. Horse manure tends

It's time to mow and maintain this pasture.

to be high in nitrogen anyway, so if you are spreading manure on the fields you probably won't need to add more. Fertilizer needs to be spread in the spring just prior to the start of the growing season or in the fall. Because nutrients won't filter into the ground and the plants are not at a stage to fully utilize them, don't fertilize in the winter or summer.

Pasture for Hay

Pastures being grown for hay will not have to withstand the level of traffic associated with grazing. The hay grasses should grow at a reasonably even rate so the bulk of the grass is ready to cut at the same time. If you are planning to use a pasture for hay, it may be worthwhile to seed with an appropriate type of grass for your area and to fertilize in the spring. After the hay has been cut, the pasture can then be used for grazing and should supply some decent nutrition.

A pasture being used for growing hay needs to provide access for a tractor and trailer and be dry enough that it can be mowed and the hay dried out in the spring or early summer. Very low-lying pastures tend to be too wet for hay growing and stay wet too long into the spring.

Pasture Grasses

Grasses that can be grown most successfully in your area will vary according to the soil type, and most of all, the climate. Horses do best on cool-season grasses, but this may not be feasible in some parts of the country. In southern parts of the United States, for instance, the summer temperatures will be too hot to sustain the cool-season grasses, so if you live in a hot part of the country, you will be able to use them only for winter grazing. For year-round pastures in these areas, the warm-season grasses are what you will predominantly need to plant.

To discover the best grasses for your area, contact your local extension service. They can take a soil sample and help you select the fertilizer that is suitable for your soil type and identify the best types of grasses to cultivate.

Pasture is usually a mixture of various plants: legumes, grasses, and weeds. Useful grazing plants are divided into two types: legumes, such as alfalfa and clover, and the various species of grasses, which are too numerous to list.

Legumes

Legumes are plants that have a symbiotic relationship with bacteria in nodules on their roots; the bacteria help them to "fix" nitrogen from the atmosphere into amino acids and nitrates. Thus, not only are legumes usually high in protein, but they also help to fertilize the soil for other plants.

Because they are broad-leaved plants, be aware that legumes are susceptible to broad-leaved weed killers. Also, excessive levels of nitrogen fertilizer will act against legumes and prevent them growing. They usually prefer neutral to alkaline soils, so in order to grow legumes the soil must be well limed.

Some legumes, such as alfalfa, have long taproots, which makes them better able to withstand drought conditions. Legumes are high in nutrition, but need management in order to thrive. In very damp, hot weather, clover (especially red clover and alsike clover) can become infected with a fungus, which leads to significant weight loss and other problems, such as drooling, oral lesions (ulcers), colic, diarrhea, and edema (swelling) along the stomach.

Examples of legumes are:
- Alfalfa
- Clover (white, alsike, or red)
- Lespedeza
- Bird's-foot trefoil

Grasses

Grasses are divided into two general groups identified as warm-season and cool-season according to the kinds of sugars they produce in their leaves and how well adapted they are to winter frosts or hot summer temperatures.

Cool-season grasses can survive winter frost and grow well in the cool spring and fall. They often cannot thrive in very high summer temperatures and tend to die back during hot summers with long periods of drought. They are usually fairly nutritious, but their leaves can contain high sugar content in the spring, which can cause problems in horses and ponies that are sensitive to high sugar (see Chapter 3). Cool-season grasses are very popular as hay grasses; however, their tendency to die back in the summer makes them less satisfactory as grazing grasses.

Fescue may not be the best type of grass for horse pastures. It is susceptible to an endophyte fungus that makes it toxic to some horses, particularly pregnant mares. Fescue problems are usually worse in the summer and during hot months. Even when fescue is when free from endophyte fungus, it does not offer better longevity than other cool-season grasses. (See Chapter 8.).

Fescue toxicosis is most prevalent — and troublesome — in sensitive pregnant mares. Symptoms are retained fetuses, thickened placentas, no milk (agalactea), and difficulties with foaling. If you have pregnant mares that have shown signs of fescue sensitivity in previous pregnancies, then the best solution is to remove them from fescue pastures before the third trimester. Feed them hay that does not contain fescue until foaling and through lactation. The drug detomadine has been successful in helping fescue-sensitive mares to overcome the toxicity and can be prescribed by your veterinarian. But prevention is better than cure, so remove mares from fescue pasture.

Fescue can also lead to symptoms of lethargy and poor performance in geldings. Again the answer is to remove the stock from the fescue pastures and allow them to eat hay made from some other grass than fescue. There is anecdotal evidence that fescue toxicity may manifest itself as thyroid problems, but this has not be shown conclusively and the evidence is anecdotal only.

Examples of cool-season grasses are:
- Timothy
- Rye grass (not to be confused with rye grain)
- Orchard grass
- Fescue
- Kentucky bluegrass

Warm-season grasses are better able to withstand hot, humid weather and are more drought resistant, but they don't survive long periods of cold weather well and are not very frost resistant. In the southeastern part of the United States, these are often the only grasses that can survive the extreme summer temperatures and, as such, are important pasture grasses and hays in these regions.

Many warm-season grasses have toxins in their leaves, which make them unpalatable, so horses tend to avoid eating them. If left unchecked, these grasses will take over the pasture after the horses graze back the more palatable grasses. Planting with the better varieties along with regular mowing to control spread is the best remedy.

Examples are:
- Coastal bermuda
- Switch grass
- Caucasian bluegrass
- Tift 44
- Brome

In Summary

Pasture turnout meets needs for exercise, companionship, and relaxation. It can, if properly managed, also supply some basic nutrient needs. It is possible to keep horses healthy without pasture turnout, but that requires excellent management. In general, horses thrive best if they get regular turnout in safe pastures with access to clean water, salt, shelter, and suitable companions.

-8-

Nutritional Disorders

THE FOLLOWING HEALTH CONCERNS affected by nutrition will be addressed in this chapter:

- Anhydrosis
- Choke
- Colic
- COPD (Heaves)
- Cribbing (Wind sucking)
- Cushing's disease
- HYPP
- Hypokalemic diaphragmatic shudder (Thumps)
- Laminitis (Founder)
- Metabolic bone disease
- Misbehavior
- Overweight horses
- Pigment loss
- Toxins in feed
- Tying-up syndrome
- Ulcers
- Underweight horses

Anhydrosis

Anhydrosis is the inability to sweat, thought to be triggered by working in hot and humid conditions. The problem develops slowly over time. At first the horse is able to sweat normally, but it loses this ability after months or years in a hot, humid climate. Presumably, the constant need to produce cooling sweat is gradually exhausting the sweat glands. This can affect both horses that are born in the tropics and horses that are imported from cool climates.

Clinical Signs

Clinical signs are similar to heat stroke. The animal is unable to lose body heat through sweating and so cannot work as well and may pant or breathe harshly after exercise. It may become uncoordinated and can collapse. Signs of colic may accompany symptoms of heat exhaustion.

Management

Many solutions have been tried. The only one so far that seems to have a beneficial effect is supplementing an amino acid mixture called One-AC and electrolytes. The exact nature of the amino acid blend is patented by the manufacturer.

Anhydrotic horses appear to recover their ability to sweat if they are moved to cooler climates or once the summer ends and nights cool down. However, this condition can seriously compromise the performance careers of affected horses that are working in hot humid climates.

Choke

Impartially chewed food can lodge in the esophagus, making it impossible for the horse to swallow. This situation is known as choke. The horse may cough in an attempt to dislodge the obstruction, and you may notice saliva dripping out of its mouth. If the horse cannot rid himself of the obstruction in a couple of hours, consider this a serious situation and call your vet. Remove sources of food and water while you wait.

Prevention

Overeager eaters that seem to inhale their food (known as "bolting feed") may be predisposed to choke. To minimize chances of choke, try adding more long fiber (sugar beet pulp is an excellent additive) to the feed ration, or wet the feed to a sloppy consistency to slow the greedy eater down. You can also place a large stone or brick in the manger or feed bucket so the horse must pick around the block and can't just gulp his feed. Don't use a salt block, however, as it will eventually crumble and it can make the feed excessively salty. Avoid feeding whole apples, carrots, or other bulky treats that could cause an obstruction if swallowed; chop them into bite-sized pieces for safety's sake.

Colic

Colic is a generic term for a gastrointestinal (GI) tract upset, one of the most commonly experienced equine health problems and a leading cause of death in horses. Colic is typically caused either by excessive gas or spasms or by temporary blockages of the GI tract, all of which are painful and distressing to the horse. Intestinal torsion, another degree of colic altogether, will be discussed later.

Clinical Signs

Typically, a colicky horse will be restless and may paw, look at his flanks, roll, and sweat. If you suspect colic, check the horse's vital signs. Assess his heart rate, preferably using a stethoscope; the rate should be 50 beats per minute (bpm) or below. A higher rate is a sign of pain. Check the color of the mucus membranes, which should be pink. Check capillary refill time by pressing a finger to the gums. Once you remove the pressure, the area should refill with color in 2 to 4 seconds. A longer refill time indicates dehydration or compromised circulation.

Use your stethoscope to listen to the four quarters of the gut: just behind the saddle area on the right and left and down on the right and left flanks. You should hear gurglings and rumblings; silence for more than a minute could possibly indicate a blockage.

In summary:

1. If the horse is restless and keeps lying down and getting up, if he paws, rolls, and sweats, check the heart rate (HR), mucus membranes, and capillary refill time.

2. If the heart rate is over 50 bpm, the mucus membranes are gray or purple, or gut sounds are absent, it is serious; call a vet.

3. Report the vital signs to the vet to help him or her assess the seriousness of the episode.

Most Common Causes

There are many reasons for a GI tract upset. The exact kind of upset depends on the cause. A few of the main causes are:
- Dehydration (either from water lost through sweat or insufficient water consumption)
- Parasite infestation (worms in particular)
- Sudden changes in feed (from roughage to concentrate, for instance)
- Over-feeding concentrates when the horse is not used to them
- Poor-quality feed (especially hay)
- Overuse of oral painkillers, leading to stomach wall damage
- Plant toxins
- Sand ingestion
- Stress

Impaction Colic

Impaction colic occurs when the GI tract becomes blocked, and there are a number of causes.

Water Is Vital

Dehydration is the number one cause of impaction colic. Because of the way the equine GI tract is configured, three narrow areas can pose challenges when partially digested feed reaches them. The partially digested materials are usually semi-liquid; however, if there is shortage of fluid intake, the body draws water out of the GI tract, and the digesta becomes more solid. If it does, there is a danger that the mass won't be able to pass through one of the narrow sections. Then the system becomes blocked by the mass, and impaction colic occurs.

To treat impactions, the vet will dose with a non-digestible oil like mineral oil that lubricates the blockage and allows it to disperse. Prevention is adequate water intake.

Monitor water intake on cold, frosty days. Horses don't readily drink very cold water since it hurts the stomach. Consequently, they don't tend to drink as much in the winter. This can lead to dehydration and impaction. If possible, offer warm water regularly in the chilly months.

Be aware that any situation that reduces water intake can lead to dehydration and perhaps impaction, such as traveling and encountering new, foreign-tasting water, as when at shows. If possible, haul some water from home or accustom horses to the flavor of a crystal drink mix or other flavoring that you can then add to water when away from home to make the taste more familiar.

Use of supplements such as TractGard, which is designed to keep horses drinking and also to lubricate the GI tract, can prevent dehydration and impaction. Supplementation is very useful during cold weather, shipping, and showing, all times when horses are inclined not to drink and thus are at risk of impaction colic.

Parasite Overload

The second most common cause of colic is an overload of intestinal parasites. A significant worm population can literally jam the narrow parts of the gut, creating a physical blockage. This type of colic usually resolves on its own, but it needs to be monitored. If it does not resolve in an hour or two, then consult a vet. The remedy is oil delivered by the vet via a nasogastric tube to release the blockage. The best prevention is regular deworming.

INTESTINAL PARASITE CONTROL

Symptoms of parasite overload are usually:
- Weight loss
- Poor coat
- Pot (big) belly
- Diarrhea
- Presence of worms in the manure

Treat by administering an appropriate dewormer. Ask your veterinarian to advise you on a suitable worming schedule.

Switch Feeds Slowly

Colic can also result from sudden changes in the feed type: for instance, switching abruptly from grass to grain or from grass hay to a rich legume hay. To prevent this type of colic, gradually accustom the horse's digestive tract to any new feed. Although changing from one grain feed to another does not usually cause a problem, if in doubt, switch between types of commercially prepared blends gradually over the course of a week or two. Introduce new grains slowly, and new hay as well.

Torsion Colic

Sometimes sections of the GI tract that are not very well anchored will flip over and create a twist, or torsion, of the gut. The symptoms of torsion colic are the same as the other kinds of colic, but the pain is much more severe. The horse's heart rate will be fast and painkillers won't reduce the horse's discomfort.

This type of colic is not preventable. In this case, the only reliable treatment is surgery. Torsion colic is basically bad luck. It can happen to any horse and is neither preventable nor predictable. Your best hope under these circumstances is to get the horse to an equine surgical hospital fast.

Other Causes

Other less common situations that cause colic are toxins in the feed (addressed later in this chapter); stress; exhaustion; sand ingestion, and overfeeding. The presence of enteroliths (stones formed around foreign bodies in the GI tract) can also cause colic.

Enteroliths are more common in certain geographical areas, such as the Central Valley of California, where high levels of calcium and magnesium oxalates in the local alfalfa form the stones. In such areas, avoid feeding locally grown alfalfa hay and rely primarily on grass hay.

Sand colic occurs in areas with sandy soil. If the horse eats the soil, typically ingesting tiny particles along with hay, sand granules accumulate in the gut and eventually form a blockage or cause a torsion. To prevent sand ingestion, feed hay and grain off the ground and give a fiber cleanser like psyllium on a bi-weekly or monthly basis.

Be aware of these potential causes of colic and prevent them with appropriate management.

Which Variation is It?

The trick is to identify which kind of colic — simple impaction, gas, or torsion — you are dealing with as quickly as possible. While some types can sometimes be handled medically at home — though any case of colic warrants a call to your vet for advice or a visit — torsion colic cannot. As a horse owner, you need to know the difference and be able to recognize the torsion variation. Have a contingency plan in place if it happens (see sidebar below).

You also need to understand how mismanagement practices can lead to colic, so that you can avoid them whenever possible. In thirty years of dealing with horses — sometimes up to sixty at a time in various boarding barns and colleges — I have lost only three horses to torsion colic. I have experienced perhaps twenty to thirty other minor, largely unnecessary cases of colic, usually because the owners or staff did something foolish. Follow the preventative practices in the sidebar to minimize the chances of causing a horse to colic.

DEALING WITH TORSION COLIC

Diagnosis of torsion colic really ought to be up to the vet. As a very basic rule of thumb, however, any colic so painful that 10ccs of Banamine does not handle the pain should be regarded as a possible torsion.

The vet will be the one to decide and to refer the horse to the hospital, so he or she will be intimately involved. But if you can't get a vet and the horse is in great pain, err on the side of caution and call the hospital. (They will want a referring vet's name, though.)

Be careful loading a colicking horse. Make sure you have plenty of painkillers and tranquillizers in him. If he goes down to roll while traveling he can get badly wedged and tear up the trailer.

The contingency plan should be:
• Keep important phone numbers near the phone.
• Keep the horse on its feet.
• Give painkiller/tranquillizers (administered by the vet or a very experienced person).
• When the vet has arranged referral, load up and head for the hospital.

BASIC COLIC PREVENTION

• Make sure the horse always has plenty of clean water to drink, and monitor intake to make sure that he is drinking adequate amounts.
• Offer warm water to encourage drinking on cold days.
• Change feeds gradually.
• Worm regularly.
• Ensure plenty of fiber in the diet.
• Feed good-quality feed.
• Don't feed grain to an exhausted or stressed horse. Offer hay only.
In a horse prone to colic, a suitable supplement can help (consult your vet for recommendations), as can wetting the feed or adding four ounces of soaked whole flaxseed to the feed to lubricate the mix.

Chronic Obstructive Pulmonary Disease (COPD)

Chronic obstructive pulmonary disease (COPD, or heaves) is developed during an allergic reaction to the dust and mold spores present in the air. These mold spores most often originate in hay, but they can also come from straw or other sources. The lung tissue reacts to the presence of the spores with inflammation, which results in mucus secretion. This makes the horse cough.

Over time, the lung tissue begins to deteriorate and break down, mucus accumulates, and the horse has a harder and harder time breathing. The lungs begin to lose their elasticity, and the horse has to use the diaphragmatic muscles in the abdominal area to breathe out. This means that exhaling becomes hard work, reducing the ability of the horse to get adequate oxygen. The result is that the horse develops a dry (without mucus) cough and becomes exercise intolerant.

Management

COPD is incurable; the best you can do is to manage it. It is a progressive disease and will steadily get worse if the horse continues to be exposed to the allergen. The vet can prescribe steroids to reduce the allergic response, but they are not a cure.

Mold and dust are the enemies here. Don't feed hay unless it is thoroughly wetted down. Use alternate chopped fiber sources, like Dengie Hi-Fi or silage. Extruded, rather than whole, grains will also contribute less dust. Complete rations based on sugar beet pulp are useful for such horses. Provide as much fresh air as you can manage. A stall is not a healthy place for horses with heaves; keep them outside if you can. Avoid working COPD horses in dusty environments like indoor arenas and be aware of their limited exercise tolerance.

This condition is best avoided by feeding clean, mold-free hay and grain and minimizing exposure to hay dust. Avoid storing hay above horse stalls.

Cribbing

Cribbing, sometimes also called wind sucking, is a problem that horsemen have long had to deal with in stabled horses. A cribber grabs a firm surface, usually wooden, with his front teeth and gulps air or sounds as if he is, hence the description "wind sucking." This is different from when a horse chews wood. Wood chewing is associated with too little fiber in the diet or sometimes with a mineral deficiency. Until recently, cribbing was thought to be hereditary

Cribbing, also known as wind sucking, is different from chewing wood and may be associated with gastric distress.

and related to boredom, but new information associates it with stomach pain from excess acidity and ulcers.

At a recent meeting of the Equine Nutrition and Physiology Society, there were three papers on this new finding: one on stomach pH and cribbing behavior in adult horses and two on the incidence of stomach ulcers, antacids in feed, and cribbing in foals.

In the first paper, by H. C. Lillie and others from Auburn University, researchers measured the pH of the stomachs of horses that cribbed and also of horses that did not crib. The cribbers all had more acidic stomachs (lower pH) than the non-cribbers.

The other two studies, focusing on foals at various breeding farms in England, were done by Amanda Badnell-Waters of Bristol University. In the first, the condition of the foal's stomach was strongly correlated to the onset and frequency of cribbing. The factors that affected cribbing behavior were high intake of concentrate feeds, being stalled, and weaning alone. On endoscopic examination, the foals that cribbed all had evidence of inflammation of the stomach walls and ulceration. Non-cribbers had neither ulceration nor inflammation.

In the second of the foal studies, cribbing foals were given one of two diets. One group was fed normal foal pellet, and the others were given the same diet, plus antacids. The foals that were given the antacid diet significantly reduced their cribbing behavior.

Management

The conclusion here is: If your horse cribs, try adding antacids to his diet. Use one of the commercial antacids, like TractGard, U-Gard, or Neighlox. Or try adding about 2 tablespoons per meal of calcium carbonate (ground limestone) or sodium bicarbonate.

If you are raising foals, make sure they don't consume too much concentrate feed. If you feed them concentrates, add antacids to their meals.

Cribbing behavior is best addressed early, as the habit can be very hard to eradicate or control once established. Several kinds of anti-cribbing neck straps are available to help control it, but surgery is the only long-term remedy. Try adding an antacid to each meal to see if that reduces or eliminates the behavior.

Cushings Disease and Pre-Cushings Syndrome

Cushings Disease is a condition most common in older horses. A tumor in the anterior pituitary in the brain causes an overproduction of adrenocortical stimulating hormone (ACTH), which in turn causes an overstimulation of the adrenal glands. These glands produce the natural endogenous steroid, cortisone. As a result, true Cushings shares the symptoms of chronic hyper-steroidism.

Symptoms

True Cushings usually affects horses in their early to late twenties. The symptoms include an exuberantly thick coat that does not shed out in hot weather, loss of muscle tissue, weight gain in the neck (often described as a "cresty neck"), soft fat that appears on the shoulders and tail head, and a tendency to founder. The definitive diagnosis is arrived at through an ACTH test or by an adreno stimulation test performed by the veterinarian.

A thick, cresty neck is typical of a horse with Cushings or Cushings-like Syndrome.

In recent years, we have begun to recognize another condition that looks a lot like Cushings Disease, but which occurs much earlier in life. This condition is known as Cushings-like Syndrome or Pre-Cushings Syndrome. Although many of the symptoms are the same, Pre-Cushings horses do not have the excessively high ACTH levels that Cushings horses exhibit. Horses with Cushings-like Syndrome often turn out to be insulin resistant, a kind of equine type II diabetes. In a horse with this condition, the cells are unable to process glucose due to an inability to respond to the hormone insulin.

A sway back indicating atrophied back muscles, characteristic of true Cushings Syndrome.

Management

The following diet is effective for both types of horses, although there is no long-term cure in the case of true Cushings, because the diet does not eliminate the tumor, which will keep on growing. The diet will minimize symptoms, but with Cushings, it is only a matter of time until the gradual deterioration results in a fatal founder attack. The Cushings-like Syndrome horses should return to "normal" and remain healthy with this diet.

Improve Insulin Resistance with Magnesium

This is what I recommend for both true Cushings and Cushings-like Syndrome horses: that is, insulin-resistant horses. I hasten to point out that this is *my* experience, and others may have different results. I have no hard scientific data to prove effectiveness, but I have fed this diet to about 700 horses with varying degrees of success. While this information and recommendation is technically anecdotal, it's supported by numbers.

Of primary importance, I recommend increasing the magnesium intake on these horses to 20g per day, or more if it is a big horse or if the horse does not respond to the 20g dosage. Ideally, supplement magnesium in conjunction with increased chromium as well (5–7 mg/day up to a maximum of 14mg/day). But magnesium intake is the key. I prefer to use Quiessence, which is a supplement that contains magnesium as a chelate and chromium as a salt (chromium chelate is currently unavailable in the United States). If you cannot locate Quiessence, I suggest using magnesium oxide as a substitute.

Maintain the horse on the elevated magnesium/chromium doses until you see a reduction in the thickness and size of the fat deposits on the neck and shoulders, which indicates a remission of symptoms. This usually takes six weeks, unless the horse is not getting sufficient magnesium, in which case it will either take longer or become noticeable once the magnesium level is increased. My experience has been that in about 70 percent of horses, quality of movement and length of stride improve, and some become more sound. But not all horses respond in the same way and to the same degree.

Once you see the horse's appearance become more normal, then you can drop the magnesium levels to 10g per day *unless* the neck starts to build fat deposits again. If so, increase the magnesium intake back to 20g. Use the neck thickness to gauge the appropriate magnesium intake for each horse.

Cut Carbohydrates

I also suggest that insulin-resistant horses receive a low glycemic diet: that is, a diet low in simple carbohydrates. Focus primarily on high fiber, and provide hay, sugar beet pulp, soy hulls, or whatever forage you can get in your area that is low in simple carbohydrates.

Add one good-quality supplement of vitamins, minerals, essential fatty acids, and essential amino acids. My recommendation of an appropriate supplement for insulin-resistant horses is the brand LinPro, which contains all the vitamins, minerals, essential fatty acids, and essential amino acids. If you can't get LinPro, I recommend feeding a flax-based feed supplement (for the essential fatty acids) and chelated minerals if you can find them, plus an adequate supply of essential amino acids, specifically methionine, lysine, threonine, and tyrosine.

GLYCEMIC INDEX OF COMMON HORSE FEEDS

The following glycemic rating should help you select appropriate feeds in a low glycemic diet.

Sugar Beet Pulp (molassed)	72.2
Dry Sugar Beet with molasses	94.8
Sweet Feed	107
Sweet Feed with oil	52

The best way to achieve this level of nutrition — assuming you prefer not to scoop from endless bags of supplements — is to provide a very high-quality protein source. Your best bets would be casein (milk protein), powdered egg whites, or extremely high-grade vegetable protein, such as canola meal. Ask a nutritionist at your local feed mill, who will usually have knowledge of suitable feed sources. There are a number of commercial supplements that supply some of these, but it is challenging to find one that will supply all of them in one product.

If the horse cannot maintain weight on this high-fiber diet, including the protein/vitamin/mineral supplement, then and *only* then should you add more calories as fat. Feed whatever fat source you prefer. I prefer fat sources that are as natural as possible, so I choose oil seeds like flax, whole roast soy, or rice bran over adding

IN A NUTSHELL

Increasing essential fatty acids intakes is beneficial for all horses, and elevating magnesium intakes is also valuable for most equids. Feed 2 to 8 ounces of whole flaxseed per day to lift EFA levels. Raising magnesium and EFA levels is also a good idea for any horse prone to founder, especially in the spring. If the horse needs additional calories, then offer rice bran and whole roast soy first and only after that proves insufficient, feed oil.

In summary, increase the horse's magnesium intake, if possible in conjunction with chromium, and reduce the level of simple carbs in the diet. Use a good-quality vitamin/mineral supplement, ideally one that also supplies essential fatty acids and essential amino acids.

quantities of oil of any kind. But if you choose to feed oils, they will contribute calories (if not much nutrition . . .).

Hyperkalemic Periodic Paralysis (HYPP)

Hyperkalemic periodic paralysis, a genetic condition, is characterized by sporadic attacks of muscle tremors (shaking or trembling) and paralysis, weakness, and/or collapse. Attacks can also be accompanied by loud breathing noises that result from paralysis of the muscles of the upper airway. Occasionally, sudden death can occur following a severe paralytic attack, presumably from heart failure or respiratory muscle paralysis. Because damage accumulates with each attack, the condition is fatal.

All horses with HYPP are genetically linked to the Quarter Horse stallion Impressive, the first individual identified with this gene. If your horse has Impressive anywhere in his pedigree, it is worth having him tested for the condition. The test uses a few mane hairs and can be arranged via your veterinarian.

Clinical Signs

Attacks of HYPP can take various forms and commonly have been confused with other conditions. Because of the muscle tremors and weakness, HYPP can resemble tying-up syndrome (see page 190). An aspect of HYPP that distinguishes it from tying-up syndrome is that horses usually appear normal following an attack of HYPP. Horses with tying-up syndrome, on the other hand, tend to have a stiff gait and painful, firm muscles of the hind limbs, rump, and/or back. Tying-up syndrome is also generally associated with some type of exercise. HYPP, by contrast, is not always associated with exercise, but also occurs when horses are at rest but excited, such as at feeding time, or following a stressful event such as traveling, feed changes, or concurrent illness.

Because a horse may be down and reluctant or unable to stand during an HYPP attack, many owners confuse HYPP with colic. HYPP has also been confused with seizures, due to the pronounced muscle trembling and collapse. Unlike seizures and other conditions that cause fainting, however, horses with HYPP are conscious and aware of their surroundings during an attack and do not appear to be in pain.

Respiratory conditions and choke have also been confused with HYPP because of the loud breathing noises some horses make during an attack.

Causes of HYPP Attacks

Initially, it was thought that this disease was caused by a disorder in potassium regulation. Potassium is an important electrolyte and is vital for the normal function of muscles and nerves. In fact, every cell in the body contains potassium; it is crucial for maintaining the cell's volume and electrical activity. High concentrations of potassium are present in the normal diet of horses, and large amounts are found in forages such as pasture grasses and hays. Regulation of body potassium is very complex and is strictly controlled by hormones produced by the kidneys, adrenal gland, thyroid, and pancreas. Because normal horses commonly consume a lot of potassium in their diets, the kidneys must excrete excess potassium in urine. Studies of kidney and thyroid function in HYPP horses showed them to have normal pathways for potassium excretion.

Subsequent investigations of muscle function by electromyography (EMG), however, showed abnormalities in the skeletal muscles. Electromyography measures the electrical activity present in selected muscles. In affected horses, the muscles displayed a wide variety of abnormalities, specifically trembling and or loss of coordination, and horses fainted for no apparent reason. These recordings demonstrated that the affected horses' muscles were overly excitable. Even when the horses appeared normal, between attacks, the abnormalities could be measured. These abnormalities were also observed when the horses were under general anesthesia and under the influence of nerve-blocking agents. This proved the theory that it was the muscles that were abnormal, not the general mineral metabolism.

Further work led to the development of a specialized muscle biopsy procedure for horses. This procedure allowed researchers to isolate and study small muscle strips in a laboratory setting, rather than performing research on the whole horse. Results from these studies confirmed that the isolated muscle was hyper-excitable; in addition, researchers discovered abnormalities in sodium and potassium levels.

In horses with HYPP, these studies revealed a defect affecting a protein called the voltage-gaited sodium channel, a tiny gateway in the membrane of muscle cells. This gateway controls the movement of sodium and potassium ions in and out of the muscle cell. These potassium and sodium ions carry a charge that changes the voltage current of a muscle cell, allowing it to contract or relax. In horses with HYPP, the regulation of ions through the potassium/sodium channel occasionally fails, disrupting the normal flow of ions in and out of the muscle cell, causing uncontrollable muscle twitching or complete muscle failure.

Subsequent studies using molecular genetics revealed a mutation at one important site in the gene responsible for sodium and potassium regulation. This mutation allows the production of an abnormal protein, which alters the structure and function of the sodium channel. As a result of these uncontrollable muscle contractions, potassium leaks from inside the muscle cell into the bloodstream, thus elevating the blood potassium concentration. The identification of this gene mutation is the basis for the blood test now used to diagnose HYPP.

In addition to HYPP, other muscle diseases also show abnormal electrical activity within muscle fibers, so abnormal EMG findings are not sufficient to diagnose HYPP definitively. Nonetheless, repeated episodes of muscle weakness or tremors in a horse — especially one whose parents also showed it or who are known to have HYPP — coupled with abnormal EMG findings would be highly suggestive of HYPP.

The Challenge: Feeding an HYPP Horse

HYPP horses require a low-potassium diet. Because potassium is found in most feeds that horses normally eat, this is a challenge to caretakers of such horses. Even when you avoid electrolytes and other mineral supplements, the horse will receive potassium in its hay and forage. Sooner or later, the affected horse will have an attack, and eventually an attack will be fatal.

Avoid the Problem

The best recommendation is not to acquire a horse that tests HYPP positive, and never to breed one. The disease is untreatable and eventually fatal, plus it is dangerous to ride or work around an affected horse because attacks are unpredictable and the horse could collapse, injuring a handler or rider.

HYPP horses are often very beautiful. The condition contributes to exceptionally well-developed muscles, and there are a number of halter horse breeders who selectively breed for it because of this characteristic. No matter how beautiful they are, such horses can be dangerous to ride and work around and are best avoided.

Hypokalemic Diaphragmatic Shudder (Thumps)

This condition, also known as Synchronous Diaphragmatic Flutter, affects the muscles of the diaphragm and restricts the breathing ability of the horse. It is dramatic, frightening, and potentially fatal.

Treatment

Speedy veterinary attention is vital. The veterinarian will slowly administer an intravenous solution of calcium borogluconate. Once treated, horses recover pretty quickly.

Causes

Thumps typically occurs in horses that have worked hard in hot, humid weather and have sweated profusely. Occasionally it happens post-anesthesia or after prolonged diarrhea. It has been reported in racehorses following administration of Furosemide, a drug that prevents bleeding into the lungs.

It was formerly thought that because horse sweat is high in potassium, the potassium lost in the sweat gradually decreased levels of body potassium. It was thought that eventually potassium levels would get so low that muscles could no longer correctly regulate their contraction and would begin to contract spasmodically. We now realize that the condition is due to low levels of several electrolytes, including calcium, magnesium chlorine, and potassium. It reflects a major imbalance in the levels of the various electrolytes.

Prevention

This condition can be prevented by providing electrolytes to horses in hard work, especially during hot, humid weather.

Laminitis, or Founder

Also known as founder, laminitis is a condition where blood circulation in the hoof decreases and the sensitive laminae of the feet become inflamed and swell, causing painful increased pressure in the hoof and separation of the hoof wall tissues. Because laminae "glue" the coffin bone to the front wall of the hoof and are the main support mechanism of the foot, this separation leads to mechanical problems, commonly including rotation, or "sinking,"

A horse with laminitis won't move and stands with its front legs outstretched and its weight on its hind legs.

of the coffin bone down through the sole. The condition is very painful and can come on extremely suddenly. Laminitis requires prompt veterinary attention.

Clinical Signs

Symptoms of laminitis are:
- Horse won't move and stands with his front legs stretched forward
- Hooves radiate heat
- Pounding digital pulse can be felt above the hoof

Causes of Laminitis

The best practice is to prevent laminitis from happening in the first place. To do that you need to know why it occurs. Unfortunately for us, there are several contributing causes of laminitis.

   1. Presence of bacterial toxins. These cause a loss of blood supply to the foot. The bacteria that live in the hind-gut can produce these toxins when there is some kind of interference with their normal activity. Various factors contribute to an overabundance of the "wrong" bacteria in the GI tract. Undesirable bacteria can multiply in the hind-gut because too much simple carbohydrate escapes the small intestine (as happens when the horse gets into the feed room and overeats grain). These toxins can also result from bacteria dying in the GI tract due to colic or overheating. Another source is bacteria growing in the uterus due to retained placenta, or from any kind of massive bacterial overgrowth from whatever cause.

   2. Interference in peripheral circulation. This causes a reduction in the blood supply to the hoof capsule and, hence, a shortage of oxygen and/or nutrients to the laminae. Interference in blood supply can result from insulin resistance or shock from exhaustion or stress, which shuts down peripheral circulation, among other things.

   3. Overdose of corticosteroids. One effect of corticosteroids on the system is to reduce peripheral circulation, and the horse is particularly sensitive to this. Both types of steroids cause trouble:

endogenous (self-producing), seen in Cushings Disease or stressed horses, and *exogenous* (overdose of prescription steroids).

4. Toxins present in the environment. When certain toxins enter the foot, such as when the horse stands on black walnut or other hardwood shavings, laminitis is possible.

5. Imbalanced weight. A horse with an injured limb that cannot bear weight can cause the opposite limb to founder due to stress and strain.

Feeding the Foundered Horse

If a founder is not due to toxemia, exhaustion, or carrying all the weight on one foot, it is considered, for feeding purposes, the corticosteroid, "resistance to insulin" variety. Feed the horse as you

A NEW THEORY ON LAMINITIS

Some current research that shows that nitric oxide is a direct messenger for many functions, including control of vasodilation (opening of arteries). Interference with, or loss of, nitric oxide shuts down the circulation to the laminae. Therefore, anything that increases nitric oxide in the lower leg/foot will help increase vital blood circulation. Options for achieving this benefit include:

• Feeding the appropriate amino acids. These include tyrosine, threonine, lysine, and methionine. There are several mixes of amino acids available specifically for dealing with founder. One challenge is that they need to be given on an empty stomach two hours before feeding.

• Applying nitroglycerin wraps to the coronary band. Nitroglycerin wraps can be obtained from the veterinarian, but in an emergency you can get them from a pharmacy. The horse versions are bigger and more concentrated versions of the ones used for humans.

• Using a therapy laser on the coronary band/foot.

• Applying pulsating magnetic fields to the foot capsule.

If treatment is initiated soon enough, all of these approaches, separately or together, can and will reduce the pain and discomfort, halt the death of the laminae, and stop the sinking or rotation of the coffin bone.

would a diabetic (see the section on Cushings disease in this chapter) by providing feeds with a low glycemic index, like grass hay, and possibly a little alfalfa hay. (Refer back to the section on Cushings disease for a glycemic index of feeds.)

Avoid corn, oats, barley, and molasses. Feed fat in the form of oil seeds or rice bran, if you need to add extra calories. Use a supplement high in essential amino acids, magnesium (magnesium is used in human diabetics to enhance peripheral circulation), essential fatty acids, and minerals.

During the actual founder crisis, don't feed the horse at all. Though there is some anecdotal evidence that giving a dose of magnesium salts (Epsom salts) by mouth helps to ease the actual attack, this has not been proven scientifically. Nor are there any clear recommendations as to dosage. Handling the actual attack is a matter for the vet.

Preventing Founder

Preventing founder is a matter of constant vigilance over both the quality of the feed and the body score of the horse. Here are some guidelines:

• Overweight horses are more prone, so get their weight down. If they are overweight, feed a magnesium/chromium supplement and reduce or eliminate their grain so that they lose weight.

• Don't overfeed carbohydrates (grain).

• Check the placenta on all foaling mares to make sure it is intact. If a bit is missing, call the vet.

• Keep the feed room securely shut to prevent unauthorized invasions and make sure lids on feed bins are locked down.

• Use corticosteroids only as prescribed to avoid overdosing.

• In spring, minimize the amount of time susceptible horses spend on fresh grass.

• Prevent overheating from exercise and bring body temperature down from exercise or fever as quickly as possible.

• Avoid hardwood shavings in all horse bedding.

• If the horse has an injury to one limb that prevents weight-bearing, support the other limb(s) with wraps or boots so that the weight-bearing leg is less likely to founder.

Metabolic Bone Disease

The term metabolic bone disease covers a variety of conditions, including Developmental Orthopedic Disease (DOD), Orthopedic Joint Disease (OJD), and Osteochondrosis Dessecans (OCD).

Development Orthopedic Disease (DOD) is a term that encompasses a group of conditions that affect young horses. These include:

Physitis (often mistakenly called Epiphysitis). Swelling and inflammation in the joints.

Osteochondrosis, and Osteochondritis Dissecans (OCD). Painful joints that may or may not be swollen but usually show deep bone lesions upon x-ray.

Wobbler Syndrome. Ataxia (uncoordination) of the hind limb or limbs due to a malformation of the bones of the neck that presses on nerves.

Acquired flexor limb deformities. Including club feet, knuckling over of one or both front legs, incorrectly aligned limbs, and so on. Flexor limb deformities need to be addressed fast, so call the vet!

It used to be thought that imbalances or deficiencies in mineral nutrition caused these conditions. Nevertheless, even when the mineral status of young growing horses was drastically improved, DOD, though it occurred less frequently, was not eradicated.

Research presented in 1994 by Glade, et al., and by Sarah Ralston of Rutgers University in 1995 implicated high blood glucose and corresponding insulin response to the incidence of OCD. Following up on this research, in a paper on the incidence of OCD and the glycemic response in Thoroughbred yearlings presented at the Kentucky Equine Research Nutrition Conference held in Lexington, Kentucky, on May 1, 2001, Dr. Joe Pagan presented some very interesting findings into the possible causes of DOD and its relationship with nutrition. Before we look at his study, let's look at how bones form.

How Bones Grow

The long bones of the skeleton grow by first forming a kind of cartilage. This cartilage later matures by forming a collagen-protein matrix into which minerals are deposited to produce the crystalline structure of bone.

The growth of the cartilage is controlled by growth hormone and is genetically determined. The collagen matrix has to strengthen itself by forming cross linkages, and this cross-linking involves an enzyme that contains copper ions. Studies have determined that very high levels of zinc, phosphorus, or energy can interfere in this process. Low copper levels will also interfere with this step.

After the collagen matrix has been produced, it has to mature before it can be mineralized. This maturation process is controlled by thyroid hormone. Thus, bone maturation is impaired in hypothyroid foals.

Once the collagen has matured, it is mineralized. For this process, calcium, magnesium, phosphorus, and vitamin D (cholecalciferol) are all required in specific, varying amounts. Very high levels of one mineral may interfere with the use of the others.

For example, very high phosphorus will interfere with calcium and may cause a malformation of the bone. Low calcium levels will also cause malformation.

As the bone becomes mineralized, it does so in a pattern. The cells surrounding the blood vessels leading into the cartilage become ossified first. If there are insufficient blood vessels going into the cartilage, then there will be areas of insufficient ossification, called osteochondral lesions (OCD lesions).

Osteochondral Lesions: Two Failures

The first failure in development is when the matrix is unable to form properly and hence cannot support the normal formation of bone. This may have a nutritional cause, such as copper deficiency, excess energy intake, and calcium or phosphorus imbalance. Problems with the amounts of growth hormone or thyroid hormone may also be involved.

The second reason for osteochondral lesions may be impairment of the normal blood supply to the growing cartilage. If the nutrient supply is interrupted, it is possible that proper bone formation may not occur.

A 1997 paper by Henderson, et al., reported the effects of insulin and insulin-like growth factors on the growth of fetal neo-natal (newborn) chondrocytes (the cells that form the ends of the long bones from which the bone matrix is being produced). The study demonstrated that insulin affected the maturation of the cartilage at the pre-mineralization stage.

The Glycemic Response

Remember from earlier chapters that carbohydrates occur in feed-stuffs in several forms. The simplest of these are the sugars and starches. Sugars and starches are digested and absorbed in the small intestine and are referred to as non-structural carbohydrates (NSC). As the sugars are absorbed across the small intestine wall, the amount of glucose in the blood stream increases. As the glucose (blood sugar) level elevates, the body releases insulin from the pancreas to control the amount of glucose in the bloodstream by causing the various cells of the body to absorb and store it. Thus, following ingestion of a meal, digestion of the starches and sugars result in a rise in blood sugar levels; the increase in blood sugar is followed shortly by a rise in insulin levels. The blood sugar level then drops as glucose is absorbed by the cells.

The glycemic response is a measure of how much the blood sugar rises in response to a meal, and thus is an indicator of how much of that feedstuff is composed of non-structural carbohydrates. If one establishes a known feed as a baseline and calls it 100, then it is possible to calculate a glycemic index by comparing all the other feeds to this to determine how much (or little) a feed will raise the blood sugar as compared to the baseline feed. For horses, the baseline feed used is usually whole oats.

Part of another Kentucky Equine Research (KER) study related to the Pagan study referenced earlier was to construct a glycemic index for several common horse feeds, using mature horses at their own research facility. Most glycemic indices used in the past were based on human studies and thus not always applicable to horses, which not only digest a little differently but also eat very different feeds. You may recognize this index from the Cushings disease section earlier in this chapter.

GLYCEMIC INDEX: COMMON HORSE FEEDS

Whole Oats	100
Sugar Beet Pulp (molassed)	72.2
Sugar Beet (rinsed)	34.1
Dry Sugar Beet (with molasses)	94.8
Corn	104
Sweet Feed	107
Alfalfa	52
Sweet Feed (with oil)	52
Timothy Hay	32

An important observation from this index is that forages — hay, mature grass (not new spring grass), and alfalfa — have low glycemic indices; that is, they don't elevate blood sugar significantly.

Another important point is that in the KER study, addition of fat to a grain ration lowered the glycemic response. So the same amount of sugar was slowed in digestion by adding fat.

KER Yearling Study

As mentioned earlier, KER conducted a large study of Thoroughbred weanling/yearlings, looking at their response to carbohydrate feeding (oral glucose tolerance test) and the incidence of OCD. In this study, they compared the glycemic response of the yearlings to a meal and compared that with the incidence of OCD. They also compared incidences of OCD to bodyweight and to the body scores of the weanlings.

On a farm-by-farm basis, they found considerable difference in incidence of OCD; one farm had zero cases, and at another, 33 percent of the yearlings had OCD. They also discovered a very high correlation between yearlings with a high glucose (and hence insulin) response and the incidence of OCD, and a high correlation between each farm's mean (average of all the yearlings) glycemic response and that farm's incidence of OCD. There was also a high correlation between the glycemic index of the farms' feed and the incidence of OCD. A high correlation between high body scores of the yearlings and the incidence of OCD was also evident.

Best Feed for Babies

The bottom line appears to be this: Provide feeds that have a low glycemic index to weanlings and yearlings that might be at risk of OCD. In a practical sense, this means forages, or feeds based on forages, and minimal grain. If grain must be fed, take advantage of the minimizing effect of added fat in lowering the glycemic index, and add oil or fat to the feed.

Keep babies lean. Remember that correlation with the body score index (discussed in Chapter 7).

Keep the minerals balanced and at adequate levels and keep carbohydrates low. (Refer to the section on feeding weanlings and yearlings in Chapter 5.)

No doubt the equine nutrition companies are hard at work formulating rations low in glycemic index for growing babies, but until they have them ready for the market, stay away from high glycemic index feeds for your babies.

A number of companies now offer "forage balancers": a low-volume feed designed to be fed with hay only that supplies all the protein, minerals, and vitamins that hay may lack. If you are a horse breeder, it might be wise to switch babies and pregnant broodmares over to a diet based on forages with an added balancer, like LinGro.

Why Forages Are Best

In young horses, it appears that one of the side effects of elevated insulin levels is a negative effect on the developing cartilage cells of the joints. The high sugar also binds with the connective tissue to form an inflexible version of the connective tissue elastin. Each time the developing horse eats a meal with sugar and starch in it, insulin rises and interferes with the cartilage. Over time, there is an aggregate damage, which manifests itself in the various lesions and cysts we call OCD or sometimes DOD.

Part of the problem is that horses evolved as trickle feeders, ideally eating continuously over a long period of time, moving as they grazed, as discussed in Chapter 1. The horse's natural feed is high-fiber grasses; they rarely, if ever, encountered grains in the wild, and if they did, grain was not in the highly refined state that we now routinely feed them.

Remember from earlier chapters that fiber in the gut of the horse is digested by bacterial fermentation, the by-products of which are the volatile fatty acids (VFAs) acetate, butyrate, and propionate. These VFAs are absorbed by the cecum and colon walls and enter the bloodstream. Because they are simplified versions of fats (hence the name fatty acids), they do not trigger the insulin response. Thus a horse eating a diet of grass and hay will not usually be exposed to rising and falling insulin levels, except in the spring when the grass is high in sugar.

Baby horses drink their mother's milk, which is high in fat and low in sugar, and eat the grass later, which by the time they are usually weaned will be low in sugar. And remember that spring grass in wild or unimproved pastures is not as high in sugar as cereal grains. They don't get exposed to any real sugar until they are at least a year old.

Adult horses are also vulnerable to high sugar levels, but because they have more digestive resources than baby horses, they can usually handle the imbalance better — but not always, as we've seen. So the bottom line is that all horses will do best on a diet of fiber and fat, with a minimum of starch.

Misbehavior

From a nutritional standpoint, misbehavior is usually associated with excessive intake of sugar and starch, coupled with too little exercise. So the best way to deal with it is to reduce the amount of grain fed and to increase the exercise, either by working the horse more regularly or by increasing turnout. If the horse is underweight and a high grain diet is being fed in order to increase bodyweight, then replacing some of the grain in the diet with a fat source will help reduce sugar levels that may lead to behavior issues.

The best way to add weight onto horses is with fiber rather than grain, so unless the horse's work load is so intense that it does not have enough time to consume the optimum quantity of necessary fiber, don't just increase the grain; increase both the quantity and quality of the hay.

In horses that are nervous and spooky despite a low-starch diet, try increasing magnesium intake. Low magnesium often results in nervous, hypersensitive symptoms. If your horse is showing these symptoms, it is worthwhile providing higher magnesium levels.

One point to consider is that misbehavior is very much "in the eye of the beholder"; one person's "high spirits" is another person's "misbehavior." Very fit horses tend to be less patient and more energetic than unfit horses. If you plan to ride at a high level of performance on a fit horse, you should get used to dealing with the behavior of fit athletes.

Overweight Horses

The bottom line is that in order to lose weight, the horse must consume fewer calories than he expends. So the best way to drop a few pounds or more is a double-barreled approach: reducing calories and expending them.

Reduce the calorie intake by slowly changing to feeds with a lower energy value. Avoid grains or sweet feeds. If you need to offer something at meal times to keep him calm (especially when his buddies are all getting their buckets), offer alfalfa cubes or a chopped hay product in his bucket. If you can't use those, try a little soaked sugar beet pulp, which is mostly water, to provide a low calorie filler. Some feed companies make low calorie feeds, usually identified as "Lite" or some similar name.

Feed only grass hay, preferably a stemmy hay without too much leaf, to keep the fiber up and the caloric value down.

Increasing magnesium levels in the diet can help too, especially with horses that tend to be cresty and have stubborn fat over the shoulders and around the tailhead. Most horses are too low in magnesium and there is no risk of overfeeding it, as it is very soluble and excess is easily excreted.

Overweight horses need their grazing time and opportunities restricted; a dirt lot or a small paddock where they can't get too much grass is best. If you can't build a small paddock, you can use a grazing muzzle, which limits the amount of grass the horse can get. The muzzle means the horse can be out roaming with his usual buddies in the big field, but still not eat all he wants.

The other barrel is exercise. Done on a regular basis, exercise helps burn calories and erase pounds. Turning fat horses out without fly spray means that the flies keep them moving and can help burn up calories. Even walking under saddle is better than standing around eating! Keep the exercise slow and frequent.

Pigment Loss

In other species (most notably cattle), pigment loss is associated with low copper intake. In horses with black pigmentation, there have been recorded instances of loss of pigmentation (strange light-colored patches that appear in various places), which was resolved by supplementing with copper, though a direct connection has yet to be formally established. In horses that fade in the sun, both chestnut and black, giving extra fatty acids and adding paprika can reduce fading. The optimal amounts are strictly anecdotal so far, but a few grams a day should suffice. (Buy the less flavorful versions of paprika, as the horse might not want to eat the heavily flavored varieties.)

Sweat is acid, and if left on the coat, it will fade the hair's pigment, especially if the horse is out in the sun. Washing sweat off after working is one way to minimize pigment loss. Avoid use of acidic fly sprays and coat conditioners in sunny weather. Or keep the horse out of the direct sun.

Toxins in Feed

Most disorders associated with toxins in feed can be divided into the following categories:

1. Toxins produced by mold in the feed (called mycotoxins). Molds can be present either in growing plants (fescue toxicity, grass staggers, ergot) or they can grow in damp or wet stored feeds (fumensin or aflatoxin in corn, peanuts, and cottonseed)

2. Presence of toxic synthetic chemicals in the feed, either through contamination by pesticides or fertilizer runoff (PCP, nitrates, arsenic, lead), or accidentally, such as through addition of antibiotics intended for poultry or cattle into horse rations (ionophores like lasolacid or monensin)

3. Infestation of feed by insects that are toxic (blister beetle in alfalfa, for example)

4. Presence of pathogenic bacteria (botulism in silage or stored feed, or Salmonella from contaminated water sources)

Mycotoxins

Mycotoxins are the by-products (secondary metabolites) of mold growth. The family includes many useful compounds, such as antibiotics like penicillin, cephalosporins, and ionophores. At therapeutic levels, these substances are more toxic to bacteria than to the animal.

Molds are single-celled fungi; they are ubiquitous throughout the plant and animal worlds and are an integral part of normal plant decay. But if the wrong species grows on a food plant or in grain stored with too high a moisture level, the levels of the toxin they produce can get high enough to adversely affect the animals eating the plants.

Some molds grow on plants in the field, such as rhizoctonia on clover, ergot on ryegrass or grain, or acremonium on fescue; these are very hard to eradicate and tend to grow even more when the plant is stressed during drought or heavy grazing. Outbreaks of mycotoxicity are usually highest from plants harvested or grazed during a wet fall following a dry summer.

If grain is stored too wet, dampness allows the mold to grow on the grain in the bins or silos and will affect the animal that subsequently eats the grain.

Accidental contamination of feed intended for cattle or inclusion of ionophores in horse feeds can result in symptoms of GI tract disturbance (colic, feed refusal, atony), heart arrhythmias, sweating, ataxia, and sometimes death. Horses can recover from ionophores poisoning, but heart damage may impair future performance.

How the symptoms of mycotoxicosis manifest depends on the degree of the contamination.

1. Acute: when a high concentration is consumed over a short period of time. This results in the specific symptoms of the toxicosis with characteristic clinical signs specific to that mycotoxin, e.g. Equine leukoencephalomalacia.

2. Chronic: when a lower amount of contaminant is consumed over a longer period of time, resulting in animals that show less specific symptoms but are generally unthrifty, look ill, and fail to reproduce, as in fescue toxicity.

3. Low chronic: when a low concentration of a toxin that affects the immune system or is carcinogenic is consumed over a long period of time. This results not in specific symptoms of toxicity, but an increased susceptibility to disease or higher incidences of cancer.

COMMON MYCOTOXINS, SYMPTOMS, AND COMMON SOURCES

CLINICAL SIGNS	MYCOTOXIN/MOLD	FEEDS MOST OFTEN AFFECTED
Leukoencephalomalacia: neurological signs, ataxia, depression, sudden death	Fumonsins/*Fusarium* spps	Corn grain, stalks, silage
Aflatoxicosis: GI disturbances, anorexia, diarrhea, hemorrhage, anemia, weight loss	Aflatoxins/*Aspergillus* spps	Cottonseed, ground nuts, corn
Fescue toxicity: prolonged pregnancy, thickened and retained placenta, no milk, weak foals, reduced fertility, low thyroid	Acremonium C.	Tall fescue pasture and (rarely) hay cut after seeding.
Grass staggers: from muscle tremors and mild excitability to ataxia and tetany	Lolitrems/Acremonium l. Tremorgen neurotoxins/ *Claviceps p.*	Ryegrass, Dallis, and Bahia grass
Ergotism: similar to fescue signs and to grass staggers	Ergot alkaloids/ Claviceps purp.	Grains and grass seeds
Slobbering and excessive salivation: anorexia, diarrhea	Slaframine/Rhizoctonia l.	Legume pasture or hay, esp. clovers

Fescue Toxicity

Probably the most common mycotoxin most horse owners will encounter is fescue toxicity. This can have insidious effects, especially on a breeding farm, as it primarily affects pregnant mares. Affected mares will have prolonged pregnancies, often with thickened and retained placentas; they may produce little or no milk (agalactea). The foals may be born weak or dead. Mares may also show reduced fertility and become hard to get back in foal.

In areas where fescue is the predominant pasture grass, pregnant mares should be moved onto a dry lot and taken off the pasture during the six to eight weeks before foaling. Feed timothy, alfalfa, or orchard grass hay. The veterinarian can prescribe domperidone as a preventative.

In non-pregnant stock, there can be symptoms such as low thyroid, stiffness, reluctance to work, and poor muscle development. Supplementation with extra iodine and thyroid has been tried with mixed results. These horses often show remission of symptoms during the winter if they are fed hay made from grasses other than fescue.

Other Toxins

PCPs. PCPs (pentachlorophenol) enter the environment from motor oil, preserved wood, and pesticides. Reaction shows as irritation of the skin of the legs, belly, mane, and tail. It can progress to ulcers and hair loss, especially of the mane and tail. In cases of heavy doses the animals will become weak and lose weight and may have a persistent cough and chronic eye and nose discharge. This condition is not usually fatal if the exposure is stopped.

Lead. Pastures downwind from smelting plants may produce toxic forage or hay. Lead toxicity very rarely arises from eating painted wood. Symptoms are a slow, progressive weakness, loss of coordination, weight loss, drooping lower lips, depression, "roaring," and anorexia. If exposure is continued, it can be fatal.

Arsenic. Sources are pesticides on feeds, preserved (pressure-treated) wood, or paints. Symptoms include shock, colic, trembling and hypersalivation, and it is usually fatal in one to three days. Very low doses over a period of time can result in hyperexcitability and excessively glossy coats. Arsenic was used in the old days as a "tonic" and given to horses just before a sale; they looked glossy and keen on the day of the sale, but later dropped weight very fast and often died.

Insects. The presence of blister beetles in alfalfa hay results in shock, colic, anorexia, depression, and sudden death; such poisoning is usually fatal.

Botulism. Silage containing small mammal remains (usually round bale or silo silage) or moldy feed can become infected with the botulism organism. Untreated deep puncture wounds can harbor botulism, as can umbilical stumps that are not sterilized, resulting in "shaker" foals.

In adults, the symptoms of botulism include rapid onset of ataxia, or loss of motor coordination, muscle flaccidity, loss of control of the tongue and tail, inability to swallow, inability to stand, and death. Horses can be vaccinated against botulism.

Salmonella. Infections can result from water sources contaminated by feces or by dead animals, with symptoms that include sudden severe diarrhea, weight loss, fever, recumbency, and death. Salmonella infection is a veterinary crisis and requires immediate attention.

Tying-Up Syndrome

Tying-up is a serious and painful condition. The large hindquarter muscles become stiff and rigid; the horse has difficulty moving, sweats, and shows evidence of pain. The condition has a number of names, such as Recurrent or Sporadic Exertional Rhabdomyolosis, Polysaccharide Storage Disorder, and formerly Myositis, Set-fast, Paralytic Myogloburina, Azoturia, and Monday morning disease.

The latest research has shown that the syndrome is actually several different conditions with similar symptoms. As a result there has been considerable confusion as to the cause and effective treatments, and a host of different methods for treating and preventing this condition have been tried. By applying various research protocols, including muscle biopsies, two underlying syndromes have recently been identified.

Equine Polysaccharide Storage Myopathy (EPSM)

In the case of EPSM, the horse has a metabolic defect that causes it to store excess glucose in the muscle cells as an abnormal form of glycogen. The excess amount and abnormal form of the glycogen causes the muscle cell to cease to function, and the muscle becomes paralyzed, which is usually known as tetany. The horse cannot move and is in considerable pain. The attacks usually follow a period of inactivity and occur early on in the exercise period. This is the classic "Monday morning disease" that was described in workhorses in years past. Following an attack, myoglobin and other by-products symptomatic of muscle breakdown appear in the urine. The urine is dark in color and smells unusual.

If a blood sample is taken and analyzed for muscle enzymes, it will display very high levels of myoglobin, CPK (creatinine phosphokinase), LDH (lactate dehydrogenase) and AST (aspartate aminotransferase). These muscle enzymes will remain elevated in the blood for quite some time following an attack, even when the horse is rested. Definitive diagnosis is by muscle biopsy when the abnormal glycogen granules are apparent.

The remedy is to reduce the amount of carbohydrates that are fed and to supply the energy in the form of fat. Keeping horses with this syndrome out in a pasture or pen is usually preferable to stall rest, as gentle, continuous exercise is therapeutic.

Recent research from muscle biopsies has shown that many dressage horses and jumpers (very often warmbloods) with chronic back pain had EPSM. If your crossbred horse has chronic back pain of unknown cause, it might be worthwhile testing them or at least trying them on the EPSM diet, described earlier in this chapter related to Cushings disease and founder prevention.

Recurrent Exertional Rhabdomyolosis (RER)

Another form of tying-up is called Recurrent Exertional Rhabdomyolosis (RER), sometimes called acute, sporadic, or chronic Rhabdomyolosis, depending on how often the attacks occur. This syndrome affects Thoroughbred racehorses and Standardbreds, some Arabs and Quarter Horses, as well as many other breeds with Thoroughbred breeding. The symptoms are typical of tying up syndrome: knotted hindquarter muscles, an inability to work, and pain and a reluctance to move. But unlike EPSM, the attacks occur in fit horses after the warm-up period. Following an attack, elevated muscle enzymes are present, but less so than in the EPSM horse. Levels of myoglobin are not usually as elevated and myoglobin is less likely to appear in the urine. The important clue to differentiate this from EPSM is how late into the work period the attack occurs.

The condition appears to be exacerbated by stress and anxiety. Investigators have ascertained that it is caused by an abnormality in the way the muscle cells regulate intercellular calcium (release of calcium ions within the cell initiates muscle contraction). However, it has nothing to do with the level of intake of calcium in the diet, nor does it relate to intake and regulation of magnesium (release of magnesium ions causes the cells to relax). However, increasing magnesium intake along with providing B vitamins helps to alleviate symptoms of stress and anxiety, so increasing the magnesium intake in these horses may be appropriate.

Fillies seem to be more prone to this condition, and there may well be a genetic factor, as the tendency can run in families. The symptoms occur in Thoroughbred fillies when they are faced with exercise and excitement; in racing Standardbreds, it occurs about 15 minutes into the jogging period. This form is sometimes evident in horses that have been badly frightened or upset, especially if they are unfit.

Handling it means reducing the intake of high carbohydrate feeds and replacing some of the energy they need with fat. Feeding such horses is challenging, because they are usually in hard training and require a certain quantity of carbohydrates to fuel the muscles. Appropriate feeding becomes a balancing act between the need for carbohydrates and the tendency to tie-up.

Eliminating carbohydrates altogether is impractical, but reducing their intake is absolutely necessary. Addition of magnesium and B vitamins to the diet may well help these horses to avoid the condition. Allowing them periods of turnout and minimizing stress and excitement by desensitizing them to exciting stimuli are also beneficial approaches.

EPSM OR RER?

The clues to the question are the breed of horse and when the attack occurs.

EPSM is usually evident in horses with pony, draft horse, or warm-blood breeding. The horse is usually overweight or unfit. The attack occurs right at the start of exercise; sometimes the horse is slow to warm up.

In RER, the horse is of Thoroughbred, Arab, Standardbred, or warmblood breeding, is fit and in hard work. The attack occurs 10-15 minutes into the exercise or work period.

Over-exertion Rhabdomyolosis

Horses that are exercised into exhaustion or asked to work harder than they have been prepared for will also show muscle stiffness and tying-up. In this form of over-exertion Rhabdomyolosis, there is considerable muscle damage and there are tears in the junctions between the myofilaments of the muscle cells. These horses require longer periods of recovery and will benefit from time spent out in a paddock.

Over-exertion Rhabdomyolosis has been observed to occur more frequently when horses are recovering from a respiratory infection and is particularly associated with equine herpes virus 1 and equine influenza virus infections. Since the inciting cause is usually temporary, most of these horses respond to rest and a gradual return to training.

Ulcers

Stomach, or gastric, ulcers in horses have recently emerged as one of the most insidious health problems. The symptoms are so many and so varied that misdiagnosis has been the norm. Back pain, reluctance to go forward under saddle, crabbiness when being groomed or tacked up, general bad temper, restlessness, box walking, poor appetite, difficulty maintaining weight, poor coat, unspecific hind end lameness, chronic colic — all are possible symptoms of ulcers. Many an affected horse has been "corrected" for bad behavior, when what he was doing was expressing his discomfort.

Recent surveys have shown that between 80 and 90 percent of stabled horses have gastric ulcers. They are most common in horses that lead stressful lives, such as racehorses and show horses, but even some pasture potatoes have been endoscoped (a tube is passed into the stomach so the vet can have a look) and discovered to have ulcers.

Causes

The reason that horses are so prone to ulcers is the way their stomachs are made. Humans have a protective stomach lining called the glandular mucosa that protects the stomach from the effects of acid secretion and pepsin (digestive enzyme); basically, the glandular mucosa protects the stomach from digesting itself. The horse (unlike humans) has a glandular mucosa lining only in the bottom one-third of the stomach; the upper walls have a lining of stratified squamous mucosa, which offers far fewer protective properties.

When the wild horse grazed naturally, the stomach always had a small amount of high-fiber feed in it, so the acid levels did not become excessive and the limited amount of protective lining was adequate. However, our habit of feeding domestic horses infrequent, large, grain-based meals and often allowing the horse's stomach to remain empty for hours at a time means that the stomach is too full for short periods, which allows the stomach acid and pepsin access to the unprotected lining.

Even when there is no food to digest, the empty stomach continues to secrete acid and pepsin. These digestive juices begin to work on the stomach lining and can gradually eat a hole in it. The horse now has an ulcer.

If the stomach becomes full to the point where the less well-protected area is exposed to acids and pepsin, the lining is a likely candidate for another ulcer.

So stomach ulcers appear to be something a modern horse is predisposed to, a tendency exacerbated by the feeding of diets high in soluble starch and low in fiber, followed by long periods without hay. Non-steroidal anti-inflammatory drugs (NSAIDs) also tend to cause ulceration. Intense training and confinement to stalls with no access to grazing or down time also predispose the horse to ulcers.

Treatment and Prevention

When ulcers have been diagnosed, the vet can prescribe one of several drugs: Omeprazole or lansoprazole, rantidine, and cimitidine are all potent inhibitors of gastric acid secretion. They will reduce the pain of ulcers and can cure them, but can be expensive.

To prevent excess acidity, you can use a feed additive like TractGard, U-Gard, or Neighlox. These provide calcium carbonate and other antacids to prevent ulcers or to relieve the discomfort if your horse already has them.

Feed high-fiber feeds and allow time out in the pasture. Pastured horses are less prone to ulcers than stabled ones. Horses with adequate hay intake, spread out through the day, are also less susceptible to stomach ulcers.

Underweight Horses

Thin horses can be roughly divided into two categories depending on either metabolism or history.

Hard Keepers

A normal horse on regular feed that has trouble maintaining weight is commonly known as a "hard keeper." Such horses benefit from additional fat in the diet. Rice bran, whole flax, and whole roast soy can all contribute fat calories. Changing to better-quality hay will also help. Check teeth to ensure proper dentition and worm regularly to reduce parasite load. Also check to see that they are getting their full share of feed, especially important if they are being fed in a group situation. Some horses aren't successful when competing with others for food.

If the problem is poor appetite, then feed more often in smaller amounts, and be sure the feed tub is clean and the feed is of good quality. Also try probiotics or ulcer antacids for a week or two to see if one of these approaches helps them regain some appetite.

Horses Recovering from Starvation

Emaciated, starved horses need to be reintroduced to feed very gradually. If the period of starvation has been of long duration, their GI tracts are not up to processing much feed, and they can easily colic if overfed.

Start with the best-quality hay you can find. Offer small amounts frequently, and gradually increase the amount the horse consumes until he eats his fill. Start with one flake of hay. Give another after an hour if that is gone, and if the second is eaten after another hour, give one more. After two to three days of the "flake an hour" method, it will be safe to allow the horse free choice hay

Very gradually reintroduce grain and concentrates. Always, always introduce grain only after the recovering horse has been eating hay for a few days. Grain on an empty stomach is a recipe for colic.

Select feeds that are based on high-fiber products, like soaked sugar beet pulp or soaked alfalfa pellets. Add in a little barley or whole oats (only a small handful at first). And put the horse on a good quality vitamin/mineral supplement.

Keep feeding the soaked fiber for as long as it takes the horse to recover and only gradually add in extra grains. Too much grain can overload the system and cause founder. The horse needs to regain the lost weight slowly.

A protein supplement can also be of benefit, but only after the horse has been on feed for a few days to a week. At this point, ideally with the help of a nutritionist, the addition of protein sources like a bit of powdered cottage cheese or egg white can help. If you can't find a nutritionist to help, feed 4 ounces of whole flax per day added to the sugar beet pulp instead. Additional fat can help a recovering horse, too. Feed rice bran or whole roast soy to contribute beneficial fat. But go slowly. Hay of the best quality is the safest feed for a starved horse to eat.

Limit grazing at first, because fresh grass is high in sugar that can lead to founder.

As with any horse that is underweight, it is a good idea to worm him and have his teeth checked before you increase feed dramatically.

RESOURCES

NRC Nutrient Requirements of Horses, 5th ed. 1989. National Academies Press, 500 Fifth Street, NW, Washington, DC 20001

Clinical Equine Nutrition, Lon D Lewis. 1995. Williams & Wilkins, Rose Tree Corporate Center, 1400 Nth Providence Rd, Building II, Suite 5025, Media PA 19063-2043 USA. 800-358-3583

Feeding and Care of the Horse, 2nd ed. Lon D Lewis, 1996. Lippincott, Williams & Wilkins. Rose Tree Corporate Center, 1400 North Providence Rd, Building II, Suite 5025, Media, PA 19063-2043 USA

Forages: The Science of Grassland Agriculture, 4th ed. Editors, M. E. Heath, R. F. Barnes & D. S. Metcalf, Iowa University Press, Ames IA.

TABLE 1: WEIGHT/UNIT VOLUME

This table is meant to serve as a guide to how much of each feed you are giving when you measure out 1 quart of feed. Note that feeds vary considerably in density and can also vary from one batch to another. So to be sure to weigh all your feed. Get a kitchen scale and weigh an empty container, then weigh the same container when it's full of the feed in question. Deduct the weight of the empty can, What is left is the weight of the feed. Write this amount down!

Now you will know what one container of your feed weighs, and you can correctly calculate how much feed you are giving the horse. Due to the various densities, notice the huge difference in Mcals that each feed will provide.

FEED	POUNDS PER QUART	MCAL/QT
Alfalfa meal	0.6	0.55
Barley, ground	1.5	2.2
Beet pulp, dry	0.6	0.64
Bran, wheat	0.5	0.66
Bran, Rice,	0.7–0.8	0.95
Corn (maize), whole	1.75	2.70
cracked	1.6	2.46
ground	1.5	2.31
Cottonseed, meal	1.5	1.88
Distillers grains	0.6	0.69
Flax seed, whole	1.0	1.54
Linseed meal	1.0	1.25
Oats, whole	0.85	1.10
dehulled,	1.4	2.16
Oil, vegetable	1.9	7.6
Soybean, meal	1.8	2.57
whole	1.6	2.45
hulls	0.9	0.69
Sweet feed (average)	1.2	2.04

TABLE 2: CONVERSIONS

Hay Conversion

One ton of hay is usually considered to be between 40 and 50 bales; thus each bale should weigh between 40 and 50 pounds. In reality, hay bales vary enormously in weight. If in doubt, weigh the bales. If you are quoted per ton when you buy your hay, divide the quote by 40 to get the approximate price per bale. Remember, one horse will eat approximately 100 bales (two tons) per winter without another fiber source such as pasture.

Metric Conversions

Imperial	metric
1 lb	453.4g
1 lb	0.4536kg
1 oz	28.35g

To convert 100 pounds to kilos, multiply by 0.4536
    100 x 0.4536 = 45.36kg

To convert kilos to pounds, divide:
    100kg to pounds   100/0.4536 = 220 lbs

To convert pounds to grams, multiply by 453.4
From grams to pounds, divide by 453.4.
From grams to ounces, divide by 28.35.

ENERGY CONVERSIONS

Mcal   = 1000 kcal
TDN lbs   = 2000 kcal/lb TDN
TDN kg   = 4409 kcal/kg TDN
Kjoule/kcal = 4.1855 kjoule/kcal

European rations are calculated in kilojoules. If you ever compare to a grain sold in Europe, this calculation will come in handy.

VOLUME

1 oz (liquid)   = 29.57ml
1 cup   = 8oz/cup = 236.56ml
1 gal (water)   = 8.35 lbs
1 oz (water)   = 0.065 lbs or 1.04 oz

Horse Anatomy

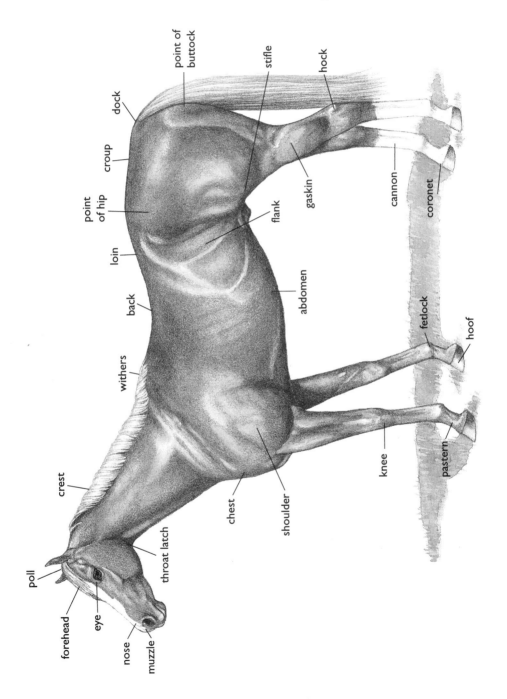

TABLE 3: NUTRITION CONTAINED IN FEED

Feed (as fed basis)	Energy (Mcal/lb)	Crude Protein (%)
Alfalfa (fresh, full bloom)	0.23	5.1
Alfalfa hay mid-bloom	0.94	17
Alfalfa meal (dehydrated pellets)	0.91	15.6
Bahia grass (fresh)	0.26	3.6
Bahia grass hay (early cut)	0.79	8.3
Bahia grass hay (late cut)	0.73	6.4
Barley grain	1.49	11.7
Beet pulp (sugar)	1.06	8.9
Bermuda grass (Coastal) fresh	0.33	3.8
Bermuda grass hay (early cut)	0.87	10.6
Bermuda grass hay (late cut)	0.79	7.3
Bluegrass, Kentucky (fresh)	0.29	5.4
Bluegrass, Kentucky hay	0.72	8.2
Brewer's grains (dehydrated)	1.15	23.4
Carrots (fresh)	0.2	1.2
Clover (fresh)	0.22	4.2
Clover hay	0.89	13.2
Corn grain	1.54	9.1
Corn oil	4.08	0
Fescue (fresh)	0.32	4.7
Fescue hay (early cut)	0.86	11.8
Fescue hay (late cut)	0.8	9.8
Flaxseed	1.54	21.1
Flaxseed meal (Linseed meal)	1.25	34.6
Molasses	1.46	9

CA (%)	P (%)	MG(%)
0.4	0.07	0.08
1.24	0.22	0.32
1.25	0.23	0.26
0.13	0.09	0.08
0.45	0.2	0.17
0.24	0.18	0.23
0.05	0.34	0.34
0.62	0.09	0.26
0.15	0.08	?
0.4	0.27	0.21
0.24	0.17	0.12
0.15	0.14	0.05
0.24	0.25	?
0.3	0.5	0.15
0.05	0.04	0.02
0.44	0.07	0.1
1.22	0.22	0.34
0.05	0.27	0.11
0	0	0
0.16	0.12	0.09
0.4	0.29	0.16
0.37	0.27	0.14
0.22	0.54	0.4
0.39	0.8	0.6
1.03	0.14	0.44

NUTRITION CONTAINED IN FEED (continued)

FEED (AS FED BASIS)	ENERGY (MCAL/LB)	CRUDE PROTEIN (%)
Oat grain	1.3	11.8
Oat hay	0.79	8.6
Orchard grass (fresh)	0.24	3
Orchard grass hay (early cut)	0.88	11.4
Orchard grass hay (late cut)	0.78	7.6
Rice bran	1.19	13
Ryegrass (fresh)	0.23	4
Ryegrass hay	0.71	8.8
Soybean meal	1.43	44.5
Timothy (fresh)	0.27	2.7
Timothy hay (early cut)	0.8	8.6
Timothy hay (late cut)	0.72	6.9
Yeast, brewer's	1.4	43.4

CA (%)	P (%)	MG(%)
0.08	0.34	0.14
0.29	0.23	0.26
0.06	0.09	0.07
0.24	0.3	0.1
0.24	0.27	0.1
0.09	1.57	0.88
0.15	0.09	0.08
0.53	0.29	
0.35	0.63	0.27
0.11	0.09	0.04
0.43	0.2	0.12
0.34	0.13	0.08
0.14	1.36	0.24

TABLE 4: FEED REQUIREMENTS FOR HORSES

This chart presents feed requirements for horses in the 800–1,350-pound (360–610kg) bodyweight range. All values are per 100 pounds bodyweight. For the total amount needed, multiply the value given by the horse's body-weight/100.

This table is a basic guide only. If more detailed requirements are needed, go to the NRC tables or consult *Clinical Equine Nutrition,* by Lon D. Lewis.

Status of Horse	Energy Mcal/ 100 lbs BW	Crude Protein
Adult maintenance	1.5	60
Adult, light work	1.9	75
Adult, moderate work	2.2	89
Adult, hard work	3	119
Breeding stock		
Stallions	1.9	75
Pregnant mare		
1st 9 months	1.65	73
last 4 months	1.8	79
Lactating mare		
1st 3 months	2.6	130
3 months to weaning	2.2	95
Young horses		
Weanling, small breeds	3.7	187
Weanling, large breeds	3.8	188
Yearling, small breeds	2.67	120
Yearling, large breeds	2.77	124
Yearling 18 mos to 2 yr old, not in training	2.25	101
18 mos to 2 yrs, in training	3	136
2 yrs, not in training	1.9	81
2 yrs, in training	2.66	113

Lysine (g)	Ca (g)	P (g)	Mg (g)	K (g)	Vit A (1,000 IU)
2	2.1	1.27	1	2.27	1.4
2.6	2.72	1.64	1.1	2.84	2
3	3.2	1.9	1.2	3.4	2
4.2	4.3	2.64	1.37	4.54	2
2.6	2.72	1.64	1.1	2.84	2
2.6	3.84	2.36	1.3	2.65	2.7
2.7	3.4	2.55	1.3	2.86	2.7
4.5	6.1	3.27	1.5	4.2	2.7
3.4	3.96	2	1.3	3	2.7
7.8	10.2	4.9	1	2.9	2
7.9	10.8	5	1	3	2
5.2	4.8	2.23	1	2.4	2
5.2	4.8	2.23	1	2.4	2
4.3	3.72	1.7	1	2.4	2
5.7	4.92	2.3	1.2	3.2	2
3.2	2.88	1.3	1	2.3	2
4.5	4.08	1.9	1.2	3.2	2

SEASONAL MANAGEMENT CALENDAR

Management and feeding routines should adapt to the seasons to meet all of the horse's needs.

Winter

❏ Water supply may be frozen; break ice daily or, better yet, supply warm water once or twice a day.

❏ Fiber is important for warmth, so feed plenty of hay.

❏ Cold and wet is much harder to deal with than cold and dry; feed extra hay in cold, wet weather. Or provide shelter from rain with a run-in shed or a waterproof blanket.

Spring

❏ Limit access to rapidly growing grass; at this time, feed extra magnesium.

❏ If the horse is on regular turnout, then adjusting to the grass will occur naturally. If the horse is on controlled turnout on grass, limit the grazing time at first and gradually increase it.

Summer

❏ Water supply is critical in the heat. Make sure horses have plenty of fresh water at all times.

❏ Watch the grass and the horses' body condition score; feed hay if the horse is losing weight.

❏ Make sure horses have a free-choice supply of salt; loose is better than a block. Feed electrolytes if the horse is working and sweating heavily.

Fall

❏ If you get a fall surge of grass, add extra magnesium.

❏ Gradually increase the hay quantity as the cold weather returns and the grass dies back.

Glossary

Acetate ($C_2H_2O_2$).
The simplest fat molecule, and a very important molecule in cellular activity.

Acetyl Co-A, acetyl coenzyme A.
An important carrier of activated acetyl groups within the cell; part of energy metabolism.

Acetyl units (C_2H_2O).
The active part of the acetate group or a reduced version of the acetate molecule.

Acid detergent fiber (ADF).
The portion of the forage that dissolves in the acid detergent solution during Van Soest analysis. A measure of the complex carbohydrates within the forage usually consists of cell wall matter.

Active ingredients.
The part of the compound that does the actual work as opposed to the inert carrier.

Additives.
Elements that are added to a feed or mixture of feeds for specific purposes, which may not necessarily be nutritive.

Adenosine Triphosphate (ATP).
A molecule that carries energy around within the cell. The phosphate groups are held on by high-energy bonds, when one is broken, say when ATP is turned into ADP (diphosphate) and Pi the energy is released and can be used by the cell to work. ATP is the universal currency of free (available) energy in biological systems.

Adipocytes.
A specialized cell that stores fat.

Aerobic.
Requiring oxygen; more specifically the metabolism within the cell that uses oxygen.

Alanine.
An amino acid; one of the simpler ones that can be synthesized by the body and thus a non-essential amino acid.

Alkaline (in regard to soil).
High pH, or high in alkaline deposits; the opposite of acidic soil.

All-natural vs. organic.
Organic means produced without use of pesticides, artificial fertilizers, or hormones, All-natural is a non-specific term that means this process or element occurs in nature.

Alpha-tocopherol (vitamin E).
One form of Vitamin E.

Amino acids.
Building blocks of protein. Consist of a carbon/hydrogen/oxygen core with an ammonium molecule (NH_4) attached. Some have special "side arms."

Ammonia NH_4.
A nitrogenous compound produced from the breakdown of protein molecules.

Amylase.
An enzyme that catalyzes the breakdown of starch. Found in the saliva.

Anaerobic.
Literally, "without oxygen"; more specifically, the metabolic pathway that the cell uses to regenerate ATP without using oxygen.

Anemia.
A condition exhibiting too few red blood cells due to lack of iron for the heme (the part of hemoglobin that holds onto the oxygen atom) group. Very rare in horses unless there is heavy worm infestation causing blood loss.

Antacids.
Salts of aluminum, calcium, or magnesium used to offset acidity in the stomach.

Antioxidant.
A reducing agent that accepts the free radical oxygen atom before it causes damage in the cell.

Asparagine.
An amino acid; one of the simpler ones that can be synthesized by the body and thus a nonessential amino acid.

Aspartate.
A nonessential amino acid.

Awn.
A sharp spike that grows out from the seedhead of some grasses.

Bacteria.
A member of a large group of unicellular microorganisms sometimes called microbes that live in the bodies, most specifically in the gastrointestinal (GI) tracts of animals. Bacteria can cause disease but most in the GI tract are in symbiosis with the animal. The GI tract bacteria digest the cell wall component of the feed and thus allow the animal to access the energy stored within. Mammals do not possess the enzymes to break down cellulose but the bacteria do possess them.

Bacterial degradation.
The process whereby the bacteria break down the cellulose in the digesta.

Balancer pellets.
Feed pellets high in minerals and vitamins designed to supply what is lacking in the hay or grass and thus reduce the need for concentrate feeds.

Bale.
A method of storing and handling hay or straw. A bale can be small and rectangular, large and round, or large and square depending on the machine used to gather up and compress the hay.

Barley *(Hordeum vulgare).*
A cereal grain that has long been used by mankind to feed horses.

Beta-carotene (Vitamin A).
Vitamin A precursor: a molecule that the body can turn into Vitamin A.

Beta-glycan (beta-glucan) links.
The links between chains of sugar molecules (polysaccharides) where the bond occurs between carbon atom 1 of one molecule and carbon atom 4 of the other molecule. This kind of bond is found in cellulose molecules.

Bile salts.
Molecules released by the liver that emulsify and make soluble dietary lipids. Bile salts are usually breakdown products of cholesterol. They are synthesized in the liver. In horses they release directly into the small intestine as the horse has no gall bladder.

Body score system.
A visual way to assess the condition of a horse, from thin to fat.

"Bolting feed."
Eating feed too rapidly and not chewing it properly. Can lead to choke and digestive upsets.

Botulism.
A neurological disease caused by *Clostridium* spps bacteria. An unusual disease of the horse. Most cases occur as a result of eating spoiled feed or silage that contains small mammals.

Brachydonty.
Low-crowned teeth that are flat, ridged, and wide for chewing, as opposed to sharp and long for cutting or gouging.

Bran.
The outer husk of cereal grain.

Butylated hydroxytoluene (BHT).
Antioxidant used in feeds to preserve the fat, to prevent it from oxidizing and going rancid.

Butyrate.
One of the volatile fatty acids produced in the hind-gut by the bacteria that break down the cellulose in the feed.

Calcitonin.
A hormone produced by the thyroid gland that reduces the amount of calcium in the blood, by both reducing the reabsorption from bone and increasing renal excretion.

Calcium-phosphorus ratio.
The amount of calcium present in the ration in relation to phosphorus. The ideal ratio for adult horses is 1.1Ca/1 P.

calorie.
With the lower-case letter c, the small calorie is the amount of energy needed to raise the temperature of 1 gram of water by 1 degree C.

Calorie.
With the capital C, the Calorie is the amount of energy needed to raise 1 kilogram of water by 1 degree C.: that is, one thousand times the energy of a small calorie.

Carbohydrates.

Molecules consisting of carbon, hydrogen, and oxygen. In their simple form they are a direct source of energy for the horse. In the complex forms they are an indirect source of energy.

Carnivores.

Animals that eat meat.

Cartilage.

The material that lines all joints and provides the lubrication surface between bones.

Cecum.

The huge blind-ended sac that is the first of the fermentation chambers in the hind-gut of the horse.

Cellulose.

A complex carbohydrate. Consists of chains of sugar (saccharide) molecules joined at intervals by a special linkage called a **beta-glycan link.**

Chelated.

Literally "held in a claw." In feeding usually refers to a mineral bound to a protein complex in order to make it more digestible and absorbable. It will be absorbed from the GI tract at the same time as the protein and won't have to go through the usual mineral absorption pathways.

Cholecalciferol (Vitamin D).

One form of vitamin D. Formed in the skin in the presence of sunlight.

Chronic Obstructive Pulmonary Disease (COPD, "hay-cough" or heaves).

An allergic reaction to the mold spores and dust in hay and straw. Causes a dry cough whenever the animal is exposed to the allergen.

Coenzyme A (Co-A).
A molecule central to metabolism, Coenzyme A links to acetyl groups to carry them around the cell.

Coffin bone.
The last phalanx or the last bone of the leg. It lies inside the hoof capsule.

Colic.
A generic term meaning "bellyache." Covers all kinds of GI tract disturbances, some of which can be fatal in horses.

Colon.
The hind-gut, located behind the small intestine and cecum.

Complete mix, complete pellet.
A mix or pellet with a high inclusion of dietary fiber designed to provide the fiber portion of the diet as well as the other nutrients. Sold for use in horses whose hay intake may be limited.

Complex carbohydrates.
Carbohydrate molecules that have the beta-glycan (or beta-glucan) linkages holding the chains of sugar molecules together. See **Cellulose.**

Concentrate.
A concentrated (low-fiber) source of nutrients. Usually means cereal grains or a mix of cereal grains but can include many other ingredients.

Connective tissue.
The tissue that "glues" the body together, it literally connects the bones to each other and the muscles to the bones. Connective tissue is the biggest tissue component of the body.

Contract (in regard to muscles).
To shorten the length of a muscle, thus pulling on its ends, which are attached to the bones. The shortening of the muscles is the only way to provide the power for locomotion and other functions.

Cool-season grasses.
Grasses that grow best in the cool moist regions where summer temperatures remain low.

Cribbing.
A habit or "vice" wherein the horse will grab any firm projecting edge or rim and gulp or swallow air. Excess stomach acidity or ulcers may trigger the habit.

Crude protein.
A measure of the protein content of a feed. The method of calculation involves measuring the amount of nitrogen present in a sample and then assuming that all the nitrogen present is from the protein, doing a back calculation. The value is referred to as crude protein, because it makes no allowance for nitrogen from other sources, such as nitrates, urea, or nucleic acids.

Cysteine.
An essential amino acid.

Cytoplasm.
The active matrix of the cell wherein the reactions and metabolism (that occur outside the cell organelles) goes on. The organelles reside within the cytoplasm, but are not considered part of it.

Dam.
The mother of a horse or other animal.

Detomadine.
A sedative with analgesic properties: that is, it sedates and reduces pain.

Digesta.
That which is being digested; the contents of the GI tract.

Digestible Energy (DE).
The Gross Energy value of the feed minus the energy lost in the feces; the energy content of the digested portion.

Disaccharide.
A molecule consisting of two sugar molecules joined together. "Di" means two.

Dorsal colon.
The second of the two big colons where bacterial fermentation takes place. Called the dorsal because it lies above the ventral colon.

Dry matter (DM).
The weight of the feedstuff after all the water has been removed.

Electrolyte.
A mixture of salts that dissociate in water. A supply of necessary minerals.

Electrolyte mix.
A mixture of the salts needed by the animal.

Electromyography (EMG).
A measure of muscle activity.

Ensiling.
To preserve without oxygen.

Enteroliths.
Stones of calcium and magnesium oxalate that form in the GI tract.

Enzyme.
Biological catalyst.

Epsom salts.
Magnesium sulphate ($MgSO_4$ $7H_2O$).

Equine Polysaccharide Storage Myopathy (EPSM or "Monday morning disease").
One of the forms of **tying-up syndrome,** where there is a malformation of glycogen in the muscle cell.

Essential amino acids.
Those amino acids that the body cannot synthesize for itself, but which are needed for protein production; hence, they must be supplied in the diet.

Essential Fatty Acids (EFAs).
Fatty acids (usually polyunsaturated ones) that the body cannot synthesize from other fats and hence must be supplied in the diet.

Ethoxyquin.
A synthetic antioxidant added to feed to prevent fats from going rancid.

Extruding feed.
A mechanical and heat treatment of feed whereby it is both cooked and expanded.

Fast-twitch fibers (Type A fibers).
Those fibers in muscles that can shorten without the presence of oxygen, and hence can function in emergencies before the cardiovascular system delivers the oxygen.

Fatty acids.
A molecule consisting of hydrocarbon chains that binds to glyceride to make triglycerides, also known as fats.

Feces.
The undigested portions of the feed that are passed out at the rectum.

Fermentable fiber.
The fiber portions of the ration that the bacteria can digest.

Fermentation.
Bacterial digestion and breakdown of plant material, usually done without oxygen.

Fermentation sacs.
Large chambers in the GI system where fermentation takes place.

Fescue.
A variety of cool-season grass.

Fibers (in regard to muscles).
The active portions of the muscle. The fibers shorten to provide the pull.

Fibrous.
The portion of the feed that is high in fiber. Fiber includes the molecules known as complex carbohydrates among others.

Fix nitrogen.
To change nitrogen into a form that is digestible or otherwise available for use; a property of leguminous plants.

Floating teeth.
The dental procedure of taking the sharp edges off the teeth so that the horse can chew comfortably.

Fluorosis.
A condition caused by excess fluorine in the soil or water. The main symptoms are mottled teeth and low birth weight.

Foal.
A baby horse.

Forage.
High-fiber plants such as grass.

"Forage balancers."
A commercial mix of minerals, vitamins, and protein designed to supply the nutrients that are usually low or insufficient in the forage.

Founder.
The condition that develops when the inflammation of the sensitive laminae of the feet has progressed to the state where the pedal bone loses adhesion to the hoof wall and rotates downwards under the pull of the deep digital flexor tendon.

Gamma oryzanol.
A mixture of sterols (a type of fat) found in rice bran, reputed to have muscle-building effects (as yet unproven). Has been reported to have antiulcerative effects.

General toxemia.
A generalized presence of toxins. Toxemia means poisoning or the presence of toxins.

GI tract.
The gastrointestinal tract, also known as the digestive tract.

Glucose.
The simplest of the sugars. An essential energy source for the functioning of certain tissues.

Glutamate.
A nonessential amino acid.

Glutamine.
A nonessential amino acid.

Glutathione peroxidase.
An antioxidant synthesized by the body. It contains selenium and is usually considered a measure of selenium in the body.

Gluten.
The protein found in wheat.

Glycemic Response.
The spike in insulin levels following ingestion of a meal.

Glycine.
A nonessential amino acid.

Glycogen.
The form of sugar that is stored within the muscles.

Glycolysis.
The part of the biochemical pathway that produces ATP from glucose that occurs in the cytoplasm of the cell.

Goiter.
The swelling of the thyroid gland due either to excess or insufficiency of iodine.

Good-quality protein.
A protein source that is high in essential amino acids.

Grain sorghum, milo *(Sorghum bicolor).*
A cereal grain used for animal feeding.

"Hard keeper."
A horse who needs a lot of feed in order to maintain his body weight.

Hard water.
Water high in mineral salts, especially the salts of calcium and magnesium.

Harrowing.
Dragging a rakelike tool around the pasture to spread manure and pull up dead grass.

Hay.
Grass preserved by means of drying.

Haylage (Horsehage, Propack).
A commercial form of silage made in small bales and sealed in a plastic bag. Usually of higher dry matter than bulk silage.

Hepatic portal vein.
The vein that goes from the GI tract to the liver.

Herbicide.
A chemical that kills weeds, usually broad-leaved pasture plants.

Herbivores.
An animal that eats plants.

High-oxidative fibers.
Fibers within the muscle that require oxygen to contract.

Hind-gut.
The portion of the GI tract between the small intestine and the rectum.

Histidine.
An essential amino acid

Hormone.
A substance produced by certain tissues in the body that acts on various tissues elsewhere in the body to bring about physiological change.

Horn.
The material that makes up the hoof wall.

Hull.
The outer covering of the seed.

Hydrochloric acid (HCl).
The acid secreted from the stomach walls, which assists with protein breakdown and digestion in the stomach. Also responsible for damaging the stomach lining and causing the lesions known as ulcers.

Hydroxyapatite.
The hard mineral formation that gives rigidity to bones.

Hydroxylysine.
A form of the amino acid lysine, an essential amino acid.

Hydroxyproline.
A form of the amino acid proline, a nonessential amino acid.

Hyperkalemic Periodic Paralysis (HYPP).
A genetic condition found in horses descended from the American Quarter Horse stallion Impressive.

Hypokalemic Diaphragmatic Shudder (Thumps).
A problem with the calcium metabolism within muscle cells caused by excessive electrolyte loss through sweating.

Impaction colic.
A painful condition that occurs when there is a blockage of the GI tract.

Insulin.
The hormone that controls removal of glucose from the blood stream, among other things.

Inter-reaction.
A reaction between substances contained in the feed. Can result in some unexpected consequences.

Ion.

The charged particle that electrolyte salts dissociate into when in solution. Can be (-) negatively or (+) positively charged.

Isoleucine.

An essential amino acid.

Keratin.

The protein of hoof horn and hair strands.

Kilocalorie (Kcal).

A large Calorie or 1,000 small calories. The amount of energy needed to raise the temperature of 1 Kg of water by 1 degree C.

Lactate/lactic acid.

A by-product of anaerobic metabolism.

Leaf drop.

The amount of leaf material that falls off the hay while it is being handled and during storage.

Legumes.

Broad-leaved plants that "fix" nitrogen: that is, change nitrogen into a form that is digestible or otherwise available for use. Used as grazing plants and to make hay.

Leucine.

An essential amino acid.

Lignin.

The woody material that the plant produces to strengthen and reinforce the stem. Consists of cellulose chains with added nitrogen.

Lipase.

An enzyme that breaks down fats.

Lipids.
Fats.

Liver.
The organ that handles many important metabolic functions, such as protein synthesis, glucose synthesis, detoxification, and recycling of lactate back to glucose.

Locking (in regard to muscles).
The condition when the muscle fibers seize up and will no longer shorten or lengthen but are "locked" in place. See **tetany** or **tying-up syndrome.**

Low oxidative fibers.
Muscle fibers that generate ATP mostly through anaerobic metabolism.

Low-quality protein.
Protein that contains few of the essential amino acids and mostly nonessential ones.

Lymph system.
The system of ducts and tubes that drain intracellular fluid back into the bloodstream.

Lysine.
An essential amino acid.

Macro minerals.
Minerals that must be present in the diet that have to be present in quantities measured in percentages (parts per hundred).

Mammal.
An animal that bears live young that suckle.

Manger.
The container from which a horse eats.

Mare.
A female horse.

Megacalories (Mcal).
1,000 Kcals.

Mesentery.
The thin membrane that suspends the GI tract from the back.

Metabolic bone disease.
A general name for a number of conditions involving malformation of bone and cartilage.

Metabolism.
Biochemical pathways that the body uses within the cell to perform all the various functions.

Methionine.
An essential amino acid.

Micro minerals.
Minerals that are present in the diet in parts per million or billion.

Middlings.
The part of the wheat grain that comes off during milling between the outer husk **(bran)** and the inner germ.

Millers Disease.
Swelling of the facial bones due to chronic low calcium.

Minerals.
Inorganic atoms or ions that are needed in the diet in small quantities.

Minimum level.
The lowest level at which a substance needs to be present.

Mitochondria.

The cell organelles that utilize oxygen to produce ATP.

Mucilage.

The tissue that produces mucin.

Mucin.

Mucus; the slippery, protective excretion from tissues.

Mycotoxin.

A toxin produced by fungi or mold.

Neurotoxin.

A substance that is poisonous or damaging to nerve tissue.

Neutral detergent fiber (NDF).

The portion of the forage that is cellulose as measured by **Van Soest analysis.**

Nitrogen-free extract (NFE).

The portion of the feed that is not protein in a proximate analysis: that is, the fiber/carbohydrate/mineral portion.

Non-chelated.

Not chelated, or not bound to a protein molecule.

Nonessential amino acids.

The amino acids that can be synthesized in the body from precursors.

Non-fiber carbohydrate (NFC).

See non-structural carbohydrate (NSC). The portion of the carbohydrates that is sugar and starch.

Non-structural carbohydrate (NSC), simple carbohydrate.

The carbohydrate portion that is sugar or starch (cell contents), not cellulose or lignin (cell walls).

Nutrient.
A component of feed that is used for the maintenance of life and growth.

OCD (Osteochondrosis dissecans, O. dessecans).
Inflammation of the bone/cartilage resulting in the splitting off of a piece of articular cartilage.

Oil seeds.
Seeds of plants grown specifically for their high oil or fat content.

Omega-3 fatty acids.
Fatty acids with several double bonds in the molecule including one double bond at the third carbon from the end. These include the acids alpha-linolenic, eicosapentanoic, and docosahexanoic, found in highest concentrations in flaxseed, walnut, and marine fish oils.

Omega-6 fatty acids.
Fats with several double bonds in the molecule, including one double bond at the sixth carbon from the end. These include arachnadonic and linoleic acids, found in safflower, corn, and evening primrose oils.

Omnivore.
An animal that eats both plant and animal tissue.

Optimum level.
The ideal level, neither too much nor too little.

Organelle.
A specialized structure of a cell, such as mitochondria, nucleus, golgi body, etc.

Osteochondritis.
Inflammation of bone and cartilage.

Osteomalacia.
Softening of the bones of adult animals due to impaired mineralization resulting from a nutritional deficiency of Vitamin D or phosphorus.

Over-grazing.
When too many horses (or other animals) graze a pasture resulting in loss of palatable species of grasses and an overgrowth of unpalatable species.

Oxidative phosphorylation (citric acid cycle, Krebs cycle).
The biochemical pathway where oxygen is used to regenerate ATP; this occurs in the mitochondria.

Palatability.
Pleasantness of taste, causing willingness of animal to eat the feed.

Pancreatic enzymes.
Enzymes found within the pancreas, used to perform the functions of the pancreas.

Pathogens, pathogenic organisms.
Organisms capable of causing disease.

Pathway.
A sequence of reactions that converts one biological material into another, mediated and controlled by enzymes.

Periople.
The waterproof covering on the hoof wall that minimizes evaporation of water from the horn of the hoof.

Phenylalanine.
An essential amino acid.

Polypeptides.
A short chain of amino acids.

Polyunsaturated fat.
A fat molecule with more than one double bond.

**Pre-Cushings (PC), Peripheral Cushings, or
Cushings-like Syndrome.**
A condition with many symptoms similar to Cushings, but which is probably a form of diabetes or insulin resistance.

Probiotics.
An inoculant of bacterial spores designed to increase the population of desirable bacteria in the GI tract.

Proline.
A nonessential amino acid; a major component of cartilage.

Propionate.
A three-carbon fatty acid, one of the volatile fatty acids (VFAs) produced by bacterial fermentation in the hind-gut.

Prostaglandins (PGs).
Biochemical messengers, used to regulate several body systems including the female reproductive tract, GI tract function, and control of inflammation.

Protein.
A chain of amino acids; the component of feed that supplies amino acids. Proteins have many functions within the body.

Pyruvate.
An intermediary compound in the metabolism of carbohydrates.

Ration.
The daily amount of feed given to the animal.

Rectum.
The end of the GI tract where the undigested portion of the feed known as the **feces** collects prior to expulsion.

Recurrent Exertional Rhabdomyolosis (RER).
A form of **tying-up syndrome** caused by an imbalance of calcium and magnesium ions within the muscle cell (not related to dietary intake of these minerals).

Reticulo-rumen.
See **Ruminant.**

Ribosome.
The cell organelle where the protein molecules are assembled.

Roughage.
Another name for dietary fiber.

Round bale.
A method of collecting and storing hay; handled only by tractor.

Ruminant.
An herbivore that digests its fiber by means of a large fermentation sac at the beginning of the GI tract. The sac is called the reticulo-rumen.

Salmonella.
A disease caused by the presence of one of the salmonella species of bacterium. Most infection in farm animals is from contaminated water.

Saturated fats.
Fats with no double bonds in the carbon chain.

Serine.
A nonessential amino acid.

Serum magnesium.
The amount of magnesium present in the bloodstream, not including the magnesium in bones, nerves, or muscle tissue.

Silage.
Grass or other forage preserved by exclusion of oxygen.

Simple carbohydrates.
Small carbohydrate molecules that are easily dissolved and digested by mammalian enzymes, as opposed to the complex carbohydrates that can be digested only by bacterial enzymes.

Slow-twitch fibers.
A common name for muscle fibers that utilize energy from fats and thus need oxygen. As they cannot work until the oxygen is supplied they are slower to be recruited and hence the name.

Small calorie.
The amount of energy needed to raise the temperature of 1 gram of water by 1 degree C. See **calorie.**

Spicule.
Small spike or awn sticking out from a seedhead.

Stallion.
Entire male horse: that is, with testicles intact.

Standardbred.
A breed of horse used mostly for harness racing.

Starches.
Simple carbohydrates (chains of sugar molecules with only a few branches and no beta links) that are easily digested in the small intestine.

Stover.
The leftover stalks and leaves of the corn plant after all the seedheads (ears of corn) have been removed. The equivalent of straw in cereal grains.

Structural carbohydrates.
The complex carbohydrate molecules the plant uses for cell walls and stems.

Sugars.
The simplest molecule of a carbohydrate. Sugars have a five- or six-carbon ring structure with many possible side chains.

Supplement.
Something given in addition to the basic feed to supply a nutrient that may be insufficient in that feed.

"Sweet feed".
A feed ration made of a mix of cereal grains and agricultural products, sweetened with molasses.

Symbiosis.
When two organisms are mutually dependent on one another. Neither can exist without the other.

Tannic acid.
A bitter-tasting derivative of sugars produced by plants in response to stress. Found in overheated dry forages such as alfalfa cubes or pellets, its presence reduces the palatability of such feeds.

Tetany.
See **tying-up.**

Thoroughbred.
A breed of horse used extensively for performance sports such as racing and eventing.

Threonine.
An essential amino acid.

Thumps (hypokalemic diaphragmatic flutter, synchronous diaphragmatic flutter).
A problem with the calcium metabolism within muscle cells caused by excessive electrolyte loss through sweating.

Thyroxin.
The hormone containing iodine, produced by the thyroid gland that controls general metabolism.

Tocopherol (Vitamin E).
A generic name for the family of tocopherols, some of which are precursors of vitamin E and most of which can be used as an antioxidant or preservative.

Torsion colic.
A severe form of colic brought about when a piece of intestine tears loose from the mesentery and "flips" over, thus causing a twist in the tract and a severe blockage.

Total Digestible Nutrients (TDN).
That portion of the feed that is digested and absorbed by the body. A general term that includes fats, proteins, and carbohydrates, but does not differentiate between them.

Total Dissolved Salts (TDS).
The total amount of dissolved salts of various minerals found in drinking water. A measure of the drinkability of water.

Toxicosis.
A general term meaning presence of a toxin.

Transverse colon (TC).
The section of GI tract that joins the two big colons. The TC has a much smaller diameter than either of the large colons and hence can restrict the flow of matter, sometimes leading to a blockage or impaction.

Trypsin.
The enzyme secreted by the stomach walls that begins the breakdown of protein molecules and hence begins protein digestion.

Tryptophan.
An essential amino acid.

Turnout.
Time spent out of the stall, usually in a pasture or pen.

Tying-up Syndrome (Tetany).
A paralysis of the big muscles of the loins and hindquarters. The paralysis is in the form of rigidity and an inability to relax and return to the resting state. The syndrome has several different metabolic causes but similar appearance and symptoms, leading to much confusion in diagnosis.

Type A fibers.
See **fast-twitch fibers.**

Tyrosine.
An essential amino acid.

Ulcer.
A lesion in the wall of the stomach or small intestine.

Unsaturated fats.
Fats with one or more double bonds in the carbon chain.

Valine.
A nonessential amino acid.

Van Soest Analysis.
An analysis of forages, designed to imitate more completely the way that ruminants digest their feed. Thus the forage samples are incubated with various detergents to mimic fermentation to assess the amount of energy they would provide to an herbivore. Van Soest analysis produces the values **neutral detergent fiber (NDF)** and **acid detergent fiber (ADF),** which are measures of plant cell content and plant cell walls, respectively.

Ventral colon.
One of the two large fermentation sacs of the hind-gut.

Vitamins.
Organic compounds that are required in small amounts to promote, regulate, and control metabolic functions. They are compounds the body is unable to synthesize and so must be present in the feed.

Volatile Fatty Acids (VFAs).
The short chain fats produced by bacteria when they break down complex carbohydrates. The horse can absorb these simple fats and utilize them as an energy source.

Warm-season grass.
A grass adapted to hot, humid summers. Warm-season grasses produce a different kind of sugar in their leaves and are often relatively unpalatable, but in the hot humid southeast of the United States and in the tropics are an important energy source for ruminants and horses.

Weanling.
A young horse that has been weaned from the mother and is no longer suckling milk.

Whole grains.
Cereal grains that are intact, as in not mechanically treated; or cereal grains unadulterated with anything additional (that is, not a mixed feed, just the grain).

Withers.
Where the dorsal processes of the spine protrude just behind the attachment of the neck and the back. The withers help hold the saddle in place.

Zeolite.
A bioavailable, silicon-containing compound. It is added to feed, as it is believed that silicon has a bone formation enhancing property. There is some evidence to this end.

INDEX

Page numbers in *italics* indicate illustrations;
page numbers in **boldface** indicate sidebars.

241

bone growth, 181–82
magnesium levels, **40,** 41, 168–69,
   170
spring grass, 66, **122,** 184
insulin resistance, 26, 66, 87, 99, **122,**
   167–69, **170**
   See also Pre-Cushings Syndrome
iodine, 50–51
ionophores, 186–87
iron, 51

J
Johnson grass, 63, *65,* 82

K
Kentucky bluegrass, 155
Kentucky Equine Research, 179,
   181–82
keratin, **56–57,** 58
kidney function, 22, 44

L
lactating mares, 125–27, 202–3
lambsquarters, **148**
lameness, 38
laminitis. *See* founder
lasolacid, 89
lead, 187, 189
legumes, 38, 66, 103–4, 153–54
   See also alfalfa
lespedeza, 66, 154
leukoencephalomalacia, **188**
Lewis, Lon D., 99, **148**
life stages. *See* age factors
lignin, 4–5, **24**
Lillie, H. C., et al., 166
limestone, 38, 84, 110–11, 122,
   166
lincomycin, 89
LinPro, 169, 183
linseed. *See* flaxseed
lipase, 11
Lite Salt, 46

liver, 11, 15, 26–27
lymph system, 11, 15

M
macro minerals, 36
magnesium, 39–44, **40,** 198–99
   antacids, 122
   electrolytes, **45,** 90
   equine polysaccharide storage
      myopathy (EPSSM), 42–43
   founder, 40–41
   insulin resistance, 168–69, **170**
   misbehavior, 185
   Pre-Cushings Syndrome, 40–41
   recurrent exertional rhabdomyolosis
      (RER), 42–43, 192
   supplementation, 43–44, 114
   tying-up syndrome, 41–43
   weight loss, 185
maintenance feeding, 118–19, 202–3
management of feeding, 95–115
   basic requirements, 102
   body score method, **113**
   calculating rations, 99–104
   case studies, 104–11
   hay requirements, 103–4
   laboratory analyses, 96–99
   meal size, 10, **15**
   measuring feeds, 115, 137–39
management problems. *See* behavior
   problems
mantua, *65*
mares, 123–127
meal, 62
meal size, 10, **15**
measuring feeds, 115, 137–39
medications
   cortico-steroids, 176–78
   detomadine, 155
   domperidone, 189
   gut bacteria, **12–13, 15**
   NSAIDS, **12,** 194–95
   oral antibiotics, **12**

S

saliva, 8, 158
salmonella, 187, 190
sand colic, 162
saturated fats, **27**
school horses, 119–20
seasonal management, 204–5
selenium, 52–53, 59
seniors, 86, 132–33
set-fast, 190
shoeing, **56–57**
show horses, 112, 114
silage, 62, 75–76, 165
size
  Eohippus, 1
  weanlings, 128
  See also weight
slobbering, 66, **188**
small bag silage, 75–76
small colon, 14
small intestine, *10,* 10–12
Smokey Joe (case study), 108–11
snacks, 93–94
sodium, 44, **45,** 90
soluble fiber, **13**
sorghums, 63, 82–83, 84
soy, 133, 195
  bran, 123
  hulls, 132–33
  meal, 16, 200
spookiness, 62, 114
spring grass, 41, 66, **122,** 154, 184
St. Johnswort, **149**
stabilized rice bran, 82
stallions, 202–3
Standardbreds, 191
starches, 4, 8, 10–11, 23–26
starvation, 196
stomach, 9–10
storage of feed, 134–36
stover, 84
straw, 83–84
structural carbohydrates, 24

Sudan grass, 63, *65,* 82
sugar beet pulp, 83, 132–33, 165, 185, 198
sugars, 3–5, 8, 10–11, 23–26, **25**
  founder, 177–78
  glycemic index of common horse feeds, **170, 182**
  glycemic response, **11,** 181–82
  misbehavior, 184–85
  spring grasses, 41, 66, **122,** 154, 184
sulfur, 53, **56–57**
sunflower seeds, 133
supplementation
  calcium, 38, 195
  chromium, 48, 169, **170**
  commercial options, 90–91
  copper, 49, 186
  electrolytes, 46–47, 90, 174–75
  feed additives, 88–90
  glucosamine and chondroitin, 92
  herbal preparations, 92–93
  hoof growth, **56–57**
  iodine, 50–51
  magnesium, 41, 43–44, 46, 168–69, **170,** 185, 192
  micro-minerals, 48
  minerals, 91
  potassium, 46, 173
  during pregnancy, 124–25
  seaweed, 50
  selenium, 53
  show horses, 114
  TractGard, 161
  vitamin A, 59
  vitamin B group, 58, 192
  vitamin C, 58
  vitamin E, 53, 59–60
  vitamin K, 61
  vitamins, 53–61, 91, 192
  See also additives
Synchronous diaphragmatic flutter, 174
sweat, 157–58, 174–75, 186

OTHER STOREY TITLES YOU WILL ENJOY

The Horse Doctor Is In, by Brent Kelley. Combining solid veterinary advice with enlightening stories from his Kentucky equine practice, Dr. Kelley informs readers on all aspects of horse health care, from fertility to fractures to foot care. 416 pages. Paperback. ISBN 1-58017-460-4.

Horse Health Care: A Step-by-Step Photographic Guide, by Cherry Hill. Explains bandaging, giving shots, examining teeth, deworming, and preventive care. Exercising and cooling down, hoof care, and tending wounds are depicted, along with taking a horse's temperature, and determining pulse and respiration rates. 160 pages. Paperback. ISBN 0-88266-955-9.

Horsekeeping on a Small Acreage: Facilities Design and Management, by Cherry Hill. Horse trainer, Cherry Hill, describes the essentials for designing safe and functional facilities. 192 pages. Paperback. ISBN 0-88266-596-0.

Starting & Running Your Own Horse Business, by Mary Ashby McDonald. This essential guide shows readers how to run a successful business — and how to make the most of their investments in horses, facilities, equipment, and time over short- and long-term periods. From general business tips to saving cash on stable management, this book quickly pays for itself. 160 pages. Paperback. ISBN 0-88266-960-5.

Storey's Guide to Raising Horses, by Heather Smith Thomas. This complete guide to intelligent horse-keeping — right for any horse owner — covers all aspects of keeping a horse fit and healthy in body and spirit. Paperback. ISBN 1-58017-127-3.

Storey's Guide to Training Horses, by Heather Smith Thomas. This comprehensive guide takes the equestrian step-by-step through the training process, from handling the foal to ground work to mounted lessons and trailer training. ISBN 1-58017-467-1 (paperback); ISBN 1-58017-468-X (hardcover).

Storey's Horse Lover's Encyclopedia, edited by Deborah Burns. This hefty, fully illustrated, comprehensive A-to-Z compendium is an indispensable answer book addressing every question a reader may have about horses and horse care. 480 pages. ISBN 1-58017-317-9 (paperback); ISBN 1-58017-336-5 (hardcover).

These books and other Storey books are available wherever books are sold, or directly from Storey Publishing, 210 MASS MoCA Way, North Adams, MA 01247 or by calling 1-800-441-5700. www.storey.com